A DIALOGUE OF HOPE
CRITICAL THINKING FOR CRITICAL TIMES

D0104514

EDITED BY
GERRY O'HANLON SJ

Published by Messenger Publications, 2017

ISBN 978 1 910248 81 2

Designed by Messenger Publications Design Department
Typeset in Garamond & Din Condensed
Printed by Johnswood Press Ltd.

Messenger Publications,
37 Lower Leeson Street, Dublin D02 W938
www.messenger.ie

CONTENTS

ACKNOWLEDGEMENTS

Our group would like to thank Donal Neary SJ and the staff of Messenger Publications for their unfailing support of our project and for their consummate professionalism. We are particularly grateful to Patrick Carberry SJ for his meticulous editorial oversight and insightful advice, as well as Cecilia West, Caitríona Maher and Paula Nolan. We are also grateful to the staff of the Jesuit Centre for Faith and Justice, venue for our group meetings, and in particular Eoin Carroll, for ongoing support. Finally, our thanks to Pat Coyle and her team at Jesuit Communications for their highly skilled and always stimulating contribution which we have greatly appreciated.

Gerry O'Hanlon, SJ

FOREWORD

As Ireland comes out of the most severe politico-economic crisis in its post-independence history, it is worth asking what kind of emancipation we might strive for and what the role of religion and critical thinking might be in a new project of human flourishing.

– Michael Cronin

In March 2016, a small group of people – David Begg, Michael Cronin, Iseult Honohan, Dermot Lane, Dermot McCarthy, Fergus O'Ferrell and Gerry O'Hanlon – came together to explore the case for constructive engagement between religious believers and secularists in imagining a 'new project of human flourishing' in Ireland.

Over the course of many meetings since then, we have come to a common view which has been synthesised in a position paper, 'The Signs of Our Times', in the first part of this book. In this paper, we outline our belief that:

◆ the modern narrative supporting the status quo is spent;
◆ an alternative narrative is needed in the twenty-first century;

◆ this alternative narrative should have input from secular sources and religious voices, from poor and rich people, from atheists and believers, from scientists and philosophers, from poets and theologians;

◆ the search for the common good in a reshaped future needs the active participation of citizens supported by a re-energised political system that supports deliberation and fosters solidarity;

◆ there is need for reflection and dialogue from many different viewpoints, since we are currently living in an axial, pivotal era, so close to the radical change that is taking place that it is difficult to see its key features.

The contention of our position paper is that there is need to initiate a dialogue that would lead to the construction and articulation of an alternative narrative in the service of a more participatory democracy, social and ecological justice, and human flourishing for all.

In addition to this summary of our views, we decided that it would be good to elaborate and clarify our position with more focused pieces on the multi-faceted crisis that we had identified. Why and how might it be legitimate to bring religious viewpoints into the public realm, while maintaining the separation of political and religious power? What might a more participatory democracy, a new civic republic, look like? Is there a way to understand anthropology, the study of what it is to be human, that can build bridges between human beings? What might a more sustainable and socially just model of development for Ireland look like? How might our position be rooted in the most appropriate slogan for our time, 'It's the environment, stupid'? And how might the Churches re-imagine a more dialogical role in Irish society? These questions gave rise to stimulating exchanges in our meetings, many of which are echoed in the more detailed papers in the second part of this book.

Our publication is not intended as an academic collection for a specialist audience. It is, rather, an appeal to all who share our deep unease at the conditions and trends revealed by the signs of our times to come forward and to engage in an enterprise of renewal. In challenging the conventional wisdom, our modest contribution could point to a 'coalition of hope', championing a vision of a society where all can flourish and feel at home.

Gerry O'Hanlon SJ, Editor

PART 1

SURVEYING THE SCENE

THE SIGNS OF OUR TIMES

DERMOT McCARTHY

Introduction

In March 2016, a group of individuals from a variety of back-grounds, but with a common interest in making a case for con-structive engagement between secularists and religious believers in our country, was convened by Gerry O'Hanlon SJ of the Jesuit Centre for Faith and Justice. We subsequently came together on several occasions to consider the possibility of forming a 'coali-tion of hope' that might contribute to a new project of human flourishing in Ireland. We have been motivated in this initiative by the following considerations:

(i)   The continuing sense of economic crisis, with Brexit and international developments overshadowing our patchy recovery from the international financial crisis;

(ii)   The alienation of many from conventional politics, the rise of populism and economic nationalism, and the distrust of political and civil institutions perceived as elitist;

(iii) The loss of a sense of transcendence in the dominant culture and its implications for human flourishing;

(iv) The hostility towards the Christian Churches as the perceived source of social attitudes that were once prevalent but are now rejected, together with the continuing scrutiny of the Churches' institutional impact;

(v) The relative neglect of religion in the public square, and the consequent inability to engage constructively with the rise of Islam in the West;

(vi) The growing assumption that religion is either some irrelevant placebo or a regressive and malign force in society;

(vii) The contemporary stand-off between secularists and believers regarding sexuality, gender and education;

(viii) The vitality and potential of signs of civic activism and courageous witness that represent creative responses to the crisis we face.

In our deliberations, we have sought:

(i) to analyse the roots of the current multi-faceted crisis;

(ii) to read the 'signs of the times' from within and without the Christian tradition;

(iii) to articulate a common position on the prevailing social malaise;

(iv) to articulate a vision that could mobilise a broad coalition of the hopeful and the willing;

(v) to suggest lines of analysis and possible approaches towards a process by which a broader shared platform could be developed for such a coalition;

(vi) to propose some lines of action that would demonstrate the potential for Christian engagement with secular society in tackling some specific common concerns.

The present chapter presents a summary of our deliberations, and will be followed by more detailed analyses from specific viewpoints in the following chapters.

Our conviction is that beneath the economic and social crisis lies a crisis of faith – in institutions, in the potential of collective action, in the State and the EU, in the future itself. This crisis of faith includes the Churches, but extends beyond them to virtually all the features of the post-war consensus in the West. It straddles the Social and Christian Democratic traditions, to the point that the achievements of liberal democracy are seen to be under threat. This arises from the apparent inability of public policy and institutions to protect populations from the negative consequences of technological change, globalisation, mass migration and the demographic transition to ageing societies.

There is also clear evidence of a crisis of hope. In part, this reflects the current pessimistic outlook for income and living standards of those seeking to set up a home, as well as for those facing retirement. It also arises from a loss of a sense of common purpose and personal meaning in an increasingly individualistic culture.

Underlying this loss of faith and hope lies a corrosive process which is disarming the social forces that are apparently in retreat: cynicism as the grammar of public discourse and scepticism as the tone of public accountability. By contrast, there are fewer sources of social capital or of cultural resistance to the process of atomisation.

The basis for this conviction and a context for the chapters that develop the themes of this survey are set out in the following pages.

The nature of the Crisis (1)

As the worldwide economic crisis at the end of the first decade of the twenty-first century revealed, the model of financial capitalism underlying economic development since the late 1970s had led to spectacular levels of inequalities of income and wealth, ecologically catastrophic forms of growth, and the dislocation of employment and income prospects for those employed in manufacturing in the West. This coincided with the apparent triumph of economic liberalism that followed the fall of Communism.

Classical liberalism, as a political philosophy, has much that is of value in its outlook. It has fostered, to varying degrees, respect for the individual, and some strands of it have come to promote human rights, an emphasis on equality, the importance of fairness within society, a commitment to social justice, and a recognition of the place of solidarity. Economic liberalism shares some of the values of classic liberalism, but emphasises freedom over equality, and seeks to protect such freedom through the independence of property and the market from government control. Thus, the positive values of political liberalism exist in some tension and competition with the dominant economic liberalism of recent decades, with its emphasis on individualism, competitiveness, consumerism, a perception of the economy as the criterion of all value, the commodification of the aesthetic, and the pursuit of economic growth premised on the myth of unlimited resources.

When neo-liberal thought became hegemonic, it began to shift from being a framework for economic policy to a comprehensive grounding for political rationality, where all dimensions of human life were to be subject to market discipline. The sole criterion for judging the success of a State under the new regime became its ability to sustain and foster the development and extension of the market. This is in very marked contrast to republican ideals, which emphasise the participation of citizens, the pursuit of the common good and the recognition of interdependence.

Furthermore, when all is subordinated to the logic of the market, humans' only value lies in their market value, understood in exclusively economic terms. Pope Francis (2013) pointed to the vulnerabilities such blind belief engenders: 'whatever is fragile, like the environment, is defenceless before the interests of a deified market, which becomes the only rule'.

The economic crash and the resulting political and social crisis seen in many Western democracies, including Ireland, over recent years has caused a fracture in the institutions of liberal democracy. It was liberal democracy, providing for generations a framework for the rise of capitalism, which delivered increasing real incomes experienced widely, if unequally, across the population. Economic collapse, gross inequalities and the failure to sustain productivity growth challenge both the legitimacy of the economic model and confidence in the political system.

However, while this market ideology has proved itself to be the 'god that failed', the institutional response, surprisingly, has not been to seek to question or dismantle a system that has generated hitherto unseen levels of inequality, greed and environmental destructiveness. Rather, the focus has been on enabling the economic model to resume its global advance. That reversion to the status quo has fuelled disillusion and alienation in many quarters, reflected in the rise of radical political challenges from right and left. This in turn has resulted in radical policy shifts, such as Brexit, and a turn towards economic nationalism whose effects may well be to induce a further round of economic crises.

The Nature of the Crisis (2)

A particular dimension of the crisis of sustainability associated with the dominant market economy is the looming sense of ecological disaster. Whereas in earlier human history it was humans who sensed their frailty faced with the uncontrollable force of nature, it is now nature whose frailty is being dictated by uncontrollable forms of accelerated growth.

There is a widespread consensus in secular and religious circles that:

- ◆ we are running out of time to save the planet;
- ◆ the cause of climate change is man-made;
- ◆ a new relationship between humanity and the natural world is required to restore some ecological equilibrium;
- ◆ we can no longer depend on fossil fuels;
- ◆ a reduction in greenhouse gases is urgent, not least in Ireland where food production poses a particular challenge;
- ◆ we need to move towards a decarbonised economy as a matter of urgency;
- ◆ we must make the transition from exploitation to stewardship – from perceiving ourselves as masters of the universe to an awareness that we are inhabitants of a world we did not manufacture;

◆ the earth is not an object to be possessed, but rather a
  gift to be shared;
◆ a particular understanding of the human, namely an-
  thropocentricism, is the primary cause of climate change
  (White 1967);
◆ the presence of so much possessive individualism needs
  to change.

The decisions taken now will affect, not just the next few years, but the fate of the planet in this century and beyond. The ecological crisis is not a passing moment, but a permanent condition that involves a profound mutation of our relations to the world – and the worlds – we inhabit.

A Multi-Faceted Crisis

The crisis which we face is economic, political and ecological, but at a more profound level it relates to the social relationships which nurture human flourishing, and the cultural and philosophical underpinnings which these relationships both reflect and shape.

Empathy

A fundamental feature of a successful democratic society is the requirement for empathy. One of the duties of a citizen in a democracy is to learn what it is to be someone not like oneself, and to be aware of the impact of choices that one makes on the lives of others. In a world of global interdependence, where our needs are catered for by people we will most probably never meet – think of the cotton shirt from India or the smartphone from China – forms of empathy need to be global as well as local. At a national level, the dominant ethos of competition and the pursuit of personal wealth and autonomy threaten to erode the sense of interdependence and solidarity that sustains the common good. Divisions by income level, area of residence, educational experience, economic sector and sharply defined personal identities all contribute to a fragmenting of the sense of a shared destiny. The capacity to imagine and understand the lives, feelings and historical experiences of others is crucial to the creation of sustainable human communities, where citizens can remain equal in their differences.

Without such imagination, the very cohesiveness of our societies is put in peril, and the ability of any country to function in a globalised world becomes highly problematic.

Digital Challenges in Public Communication

Profound changes in communication, and hence in how public discourse develops, are occurring as a result of the rise of social media. It has become clear how the power of negative messages in tweets and social media generally has eroded civil discourse. Many have taken the licence to say what was hitherto unsayable, and this has given rise to fear and hate. This has been exemplified in the Brexit referendum, in the 2016 Presidential election in the USA, and in how the migration/refugee crisis has been framed in many EU countries. The fragmentation of media has supported the rise of communities of the like-minded, frequently defined by their hostility to others with whom communication, where it occurs, tends to reinforce distance and stereotypes. The properly high value placed on freedom of expression has produced, through new forms of media, a world of voice without dialogue. This has called into question how the narrative of news stories gets framed and points to the importance of media literacy and media education. The digital age challenges us to consider how the new media can support proper public deliberation and not destroy democratic culture.

Responsibility

There is a widespread perception that a clear sense of responsibility for events that have shaken economic, political and social relationships has been absent. The result is a perception of consequences without causes; nobody, it seems, is to blame, and yet the mass of citizens have had to pay the cost. This, in turn, leads to an understandable and widespread discrediting of all authority, compounded by a social fragmentation which, in turn, is amplified by the immediacy and personalisation of communications media.

The absence of a more considered debate and a more inclusive deliberation on economic and political challenges can produce damaging effects. The consumerist materialism, which was widespread during the Celtic Tiger years, may have been one such consequence. A lack of clarity about values, goals, aims and objectives often results in an uncritical response to emerging trends; these trends can arise within organisations or in the wider society, and may be prompted by senior figures in the public or private sectors, by media commentators or by the more anonymous manifestations of commercial pressure. In addition, when ideas are left unexamined, the temptation is to treat politics as all about 'them and us', where personalities are everything, and policies are either downplayed or framed primarily for sectional advantage.

Enforced Conventional Wisdom

The strength of conventional wisdom, anchored in the dominant logic of the market and reinforced by pervasive media narratives, simplifies social reality and encourages the view that there is no alternative to whatever is seen as technically necessary or most convenient for a 'modern society'.

Experience teaches that the search for understanding is, above all, an initiation into unsuspected complexity. The simplest of situations involving other humans often turns out to be not as straightforward as first thought. What this schooling in complexity reveals is the radical insufficiency of cultural shorthand. Once people are described using conventional labels, the label suggests that one has understood all one needs to know. The label makes the person fully transparent, as it were. Thus, for example, those who are categorised as 'Muslim' or 'Catholic' must be, by definition, bigoted, anti-modern, misogynist and obscurantist.

Education

Given the power of the education system as a shaper and transmitter of knowledge, attitudes, beliefs and values, the scale of the crisis facing Western society necessarily entails consideration of the type of educational system that acts as a carrier of these traits.

Current policy and practice asserts that teaching inputs and learning outputs can be measured, and that the results of these measurements can be taken as indicative of quality, excellence in teaching, and the value of research. However, there is much in education that cannot be counted and that is of crucial importance, such as the appreciation of beauty, the commitment to truth and goodness, and the exercise of imagination, memory and empathy. How is the development of the interior life, that is of key importance to all human beings, to be measured, or is it no longer to be considered a goal of education?

Public policy towards education in western societies is in danger of transforming it into a commodity, a productive business, where students and parents are perceived as clients and customers respectively, teachers as functionaries, and principals as managers. Expressions of this tendency in education can be found in the race for points for entry into third-level institutions, in the growth of grind schools, and in the mechanical measuring of outcomes through simplified scores and league tables.

What it Means to be Human

The scale of the challenges faced by society, including the profound challenges to the achievements of human culture, make it imperative to work out and articulate a new understanding of what it is to be human in the modern world. Anthropology – the study of what it means to be human – is more often than not taken for granted and its foundations unquestioned. Yet quite distinct approaches are reflected in different areas of life and study which shape our culture. For example, ethics can be built around utilitarian values and expressivist individualism. Education policy may ignore the human qualities of interiority, subjectivity and consciousness. An excessively anthropocentric ecology sees the human as the measure of everything, with the risk that the human may become disconnected from nature. The pursuit of human flourishing requires a clear sense of what it means to be human.

The Challenges in Ireland

The issues raised here have general application across the Western World. There are, however, particular expressions of these phenomena in Ireland which pose specific challenges here. Ireland has gone through a boom-and-bust cycle, leaving in its wake an unequal society, and an increasing number of people alienated from democratic institutions and political processes.

A sense of vulnerability has continued as international and domestic events have unfolded over the recent past. Recent challenges to the corporation tax regime have served as a reminder that the economic strategy of reliance on attracting mainly US corporations to base themselves here, while hugely successful, entails major vulnerabilities. This sense of economic fragility has been compounded by the outcome of the Brexit referendum, which poses risks to both current and traditional trade and investment channels. It also raises the particular difficulties of a potential 'hard' EU border regime on the island. The persistence and deepening of the housing crisis has produced a grotesque crisis of homelessness, while putting the long-established pattern of home ownership beyond the capacity of young families.

A number of questions arise from these realities. Have we learnt anything from the boom-and-bust experience? Is there an appetite to question the underlying assumptions driving the economy? Will the 'new politics' or the 'progressive politics' deliver a more participative democracy and a more just society? Or will people simply suffer on in the same way in terms of the social, political and economic status quo?

The whole-hearted engagement of so many people in the 1916 Centenary Programme, which not only produced creative acts of commemoration but in many cases evoked reflection on current circumstances, suggests both an appetite and a capacity for critical thinking. As Ireland comes out of the most severe politico-economic crisis in its post-independence history, it is worth asking what kind of emancipation we might strive for and, in particular, what the role of religion and critical thinking might be in a new project of human flourishing.

There is an onus on all of those with a concern for justice and the common good to contribute to the search for a better way to organise our common life, so as to respect human dignity and better facilitate human flourishing. Christians in particular understand that they have a duty to advance the liberation of people through the progressive realisation of the Kingdom proclaimed by Jesus. Christians believe that they bring 'Good News' for human society in all ages and situations. The conviction that God loves his people – all people – and has engaged directly in human history, securing the ultimate victory of life over death and good over evil, has implications for how the task of organising social arrangements should be approached. In particular, it points to the central importance of human dignity, priority for the poor and the vulnerable, and respect for creation of which humanity forms but a part. Standing aside from the political, social, economic and cultural challenges of our day is not an option for the Christian, or for Christian Churches.

The Changing Role of the Churches

The Churches come to these challenges not as detached observers, but as institutions and communities that are wholly engaged. They witness in themselves the issues with which the wider society must grapple. They are wounded and, in the eyes of many, discredited. Their exercise of institutional power has been as flawed and destructive as that of any civil or political institution. Behaviour that betrayed the central tenets of the Kingdom preached by Jesus arguably has represented a greater failure than any in the civil domain.

So, it is in brokenness and humiliation, as much as in proclamation of a Kingdom often betrayed, that the Churches enter into the current public discourse. A potentially key contribution to the debate will involve the Churches' own reflection on how their role in Irish society developed as it did, and how institutional logic and vested interest can exact a terrible human price. Indeed, such reflection is the price of their admission.

The Christian Churches have a particular responsibility to contribute to the ongoing search for reconciliation, truth and justice on the island of Ireland, given the continuing reality of sectarianism and the legacy of bitter struggles which is reflected in polarised politics and divided communities in Northern Ireland. The Churches face the challenge of being reconciled themselves in order to make a more effective contribution to the wider society. With its extensive presence, long history of social engagement and espousal of integral human development, the Catholic Church in Ireland has a particular responsibility and opportunity to contribute to the response to the crisis in society.

The significance of the Catholic perspective has been acknowledged from the outside, so to speak – for example by Joe Humphreys (2016a) in *The Irish Times*:

> The Catholic Church is one of the only institutions in Irish society that talks about fundamental values, meaning and human purpose ... The Catholic Church also serves a particular purpose in Ireland by providing the basic unity of community ... The

parish remains the key identifier around which sports clubs, fundraising efforts, political campaigning and educational activities typically revolve. It is also the place towards which many people gravitate to commemorate important events like birth, marriage and death.

For those seeking greater justice and more humane social and cultural conditions from a secular perspective, this poses a challenge articulated by Humphreys:

Should one try to dismantle existing community bonds in order to build a better and fairer society? Or should one work with Church bodies to try to achieve the same goal?

Humphreys has also pointed to the powerful capacity of an appeal to values which resonate with the Christian perspective on social life – compassion, charity, humility and justice – in order to mobilise public support for political action. Moreover, he has pointed (2016b) to the significant leadership role of religiously identified personalities in promoting social reform and political change. He quotes Ronald Dworkin, the American philosopher, in arguing that political progressives should cultivate a religious attitude in asserting the intrinsic value of human life and of nature itself, as a framework for engagement across the wide spectrum of issues entailed in human flourishing.

The depth of recent scandals and the vehemence of the public revulsion at their disclosure, despite the passage of time and the scale of social change in the interim, may have shaken the social attachment to which Humphreys referred. Yet it seems likely that the anger and rejection focused on the Church at national level may be less evident in attitudes to parish and the local ec-clesial presence. In any event, the role of the Churches is rapid-ly changing from one of institutional power to movements with civic importance, from being at the centre of 'the establishment' to marginalisation in popular culture, and from privilege to the uncertain status of plurality. While these changes are deeply chal-lenging to traditional understanding and behaviour, they create the need and opportunity to establish new forms of engagement with the changing society of which they form a part.

The challenge therefore is as much to Christians and to the Churches as it is to secular progressives contemplating Ireland's current malaise. As Archbishop Diarmuid Martin (2016a) has put it in a homily in the Mater Dei Institute:

> We need to look at understanding what faith means in today's society; what prayer means in a society which finds itself uncertain in understanding the transcendent, and which results in that sensitivity and caring outreach to the old and new peripheries of society which Pope Francis calls for.

This implies overcoming barriers created by stereotypes, resulting often in a kind of Punch-and-Judy show of the 'ancients' and the 'moderns', in which the enemy is alternatively the godless or the God-fearing Other. The effect of this false dichotomy is to con-ceal the very considerable overlap in concerns and values between believers and progressive secularists.

Shared Perspectives and Guiding Principles

A realignment in response to current challenges could be built upon substantial points of engagement, through key concepts which are central to many forms of religious belief and progressive politics. This could amount to a new 'coalition of the willing' dedicated to the construction of a free, humane, meaningful and spiritually transformed polity and educational system.

These shared perspectives could provide a set of guiding principles in the framing of this new approach:

◆ that the modern narrative supporting the status quo is spent;

◆ that an alternative narrative is needed in the twenty-first century;

◆ that this alternative should have input from secular sources and religious voices, from poor people and rich people, from atheists and believers, from scientists and philosophers, from poets and theologians;

◆ that the search for the common good in a reshaped future needs the active participation of citizens supported by a re-energised political system that supports deliberation and fosters solidarity;

◆ that we are currently living in an axial era where, in the midst of radical change, we are so close to it that we cannot see it clearly.

These principles suggest the potential for this broad coalition of the willing to engage with the urgent need:

◆ to reimagine the human enterprise from the bottom up, as well as from the top down;

◆ to look at the human condition from the inside out as well as the outside in, at the possibility of an interior life alongside the importance of a social life;

◆ to form a coalition of voices to express the unease that

so many feel and experience with the status quo;

◆ to articulate what alternative narratives might look like.

The contention of our group is that there is a need to initiate a dialogue that would lead to the construction and articulation of an alternative narrative in the service of a more participative democracy, social and ecological justice, and human flourishing for all.

Shaping a New Vision

Citizens come into the 'public square' from many ethnic, cultural, religious and secular backgrounds. The challenge is collectively to imagine, describe and agree what comprises a flourishing society.

Some reimagining exercises have occurred in Ireland already, for example, *On the Importance of Ethics: A Report on the President of Ireland's Ethics Initiative* (2016) and *Citizens Rising: A Report from the People's Conversation* (2015). The latter sets out common themes and five key challenges from over thirty conversations in fifteen different civil society organisations. The challenges which emerged were:

◆ Increasing participation in public decision making;

◆ Developing and nurturing active citizenship;

◆ Building trust and respect;

◆ Making citizenship global;

◆ Resourcing and empowering citizens.

It would seem from these and other examples that there is a yearning for a more truly civic republican society and state in Ireland.

In the light of this experience, the first element in developing a common vision of the type proposed here may be one of creating a new 'civic public square'. Grounded in democratic and republican principles, such a civic public square would recognise that Churches and faith communities have both the right and the opportunity to express their faith-informed views in public, and to participate in debate, deliberation and decisions taken by democratic organs in pursuit of the common good.

Public life is open to be informed and shaped by citizens of all faiths, where they reason together with those of no religious faith about the meaning of the good life and the common good. Such engagement facilitates moral and spiritual questions to be taken seriously as they bear upon broad social, economic and civic concerns. The civic public square demands of all, including the Churches, that their contributions should provide evidence, give reasons that serve the common good, and are accessible to deliberation and debate for those who do not share any particular faith commitment.

In the institutional Churches in Ireland today, there are many outward-directed initiatives engaged with the social malaise described in this chapter, e.g. bodies devoted to faith and justice, networks concerned with service delivery, and those engaged in pastoral strategy. Reflection on the situation prompts the question: how can so much effort and such strong traditions be so marginal to contemporary Irish public discourse and consciousness? It may be that they have to develop a new language and mode of engagement if they are to be heard in the public square. An alternative vision, then, needs to be imbued with democratic and republican ideals which will foster the freedom, equality and fulfilment of every person and seek to ensure that the common good is the lodestar of all public policies and actions.

Giving Expression to the New vision

If, as Pope Francis (2013) says, 'time is greater than space' – meaning that, in seeking change, priority should be given to initiating processes that over time will bear fruit in significant historical events rather than expecting immediate results – then there is a case for creating and strengthening pools of creativity and resistance to the prevailing alienation. An opportunity exists for faith communities – for example, in parishes, projects and services – to engage more systematically with like-minded actors in civil society, including public agencies, in positive action to affirm human dignity and express solidarity. The emphasis would be on actions which directly impinge on barriers to human flourishing and which challenge the instrumental anthropology of the market. Such actions would discover, strengthen and affirm the capacity for positive action that challenges the conventional wisdom. They could include initiatives in respect of community development, homelessness, community mental health, public engagement in policy-making, as well as the cross-cutting issues of ethics, education and ecology.

Such local action may be regarded, literally, as parochial, while many of the issues to be confronted have roots which appear to be systemic or global. Such efforts can be powerful, however, since it is the local connection which makes possible the ethical imagining of action to address global challenges. Local action can become a highly effective form of mobilisation by starting from concrete, near-to-hand examples in addressing issues that have a resonance beyond a specific locale. The movement inwards is an opening up, not a shutting down.

As a result, apparently limited local action can be the means of significant social change. Malcolm Gladwell's work (2002) has highlighted that micro-shifts – small changes brought about by the actions of a relatively small number of individuals – can have significant effects. Assuming a powerlessness of the local, in contrast to the overwhelming force of the global, may be to misunderstand the nature of change.

The type of initiative described here would, in many cases, represent a continuation of a long history by parishes, religious orders and associations of Christians in providing services to the community. What would characterise this new approach would be a conscious placing of the resources of the Churches at the service of society, especially the poorest and most vulnerable, rather than promoting their own interests or advancement.

For example, where denominational national schools have demonstrated the capacity to welcome a wide diversity of enrolment, in terms of both national and religious identity, their adaptation to meet this need can be of great importance in the service of integration and social harmony. Parish communities in disadvantaged areas, both urban and rural, are often the only community-based organisations with premises and personnel which are committed exclusively to the service of that local community. Their capacity to stand with the whole community and empower them to articulate their needs and organise themselves to address them – directly and in partnership with public bodies – can be a powerful witness to progressive values, as well as an effective response to specific needs.

Social engagement, especially in ways that challenge the logic of the market, may be an especially rich context for ecumenical encounter. Churches working together and deploying their people and premises in response to need may enhance social effectiveness while promoting reconciliation and a framework for interfaith cooperation with the new communities who will live their faith as part of a diversifying Irish society. This would be a particular benefit of the broad coalition of both faith-based and other initiatives which is advocated in this chapter.

A National Dialogue

In parallel with the activism that mobilises those committed to the common good at local level, there are a number of areas where broadly based reflection would offer significant promise, not least because they provide an important platform for dialogue on which secularists and religious people, believers and unbelievers, can enter into a meaningful conversation. They could lead to a re-positioning of public discourse and a reappraisal of the trajectory of economic and political life.

These areas, a summary of which is given below, are further developed in the chapters which follow.

The first is the debate about **ethics** and the ethical dimension of Irish life. President Michael D. Higgins, as part of a programme in DCU entitled 'Ethics for All', has spoken (2013) about the need for an ethical economy. This is a theme he has touched on in a variety of places, as he calls for a new ethical approach to economic policy and practice. In DCU, he pointed out 'that the presence of a culture devoid of ethics in many of our institutions … played a key role in our nation's loss of prosperity and economic sovereignty'.

A reinvigoration of that debate, with an articulation of specific challenges for particular facets of Irish life and institutions, would provide rich material for a robust critique of much that inhibits human flourishing.

Another area we wish to highlight is the broad field of **education**. While much has been said about the denominational profile of schools, less is heard about the emerging impact of curricular reform. Much of this is built on a certain anthropological reductionism, where the human is reduced to the level of making mechanical or robotic responses to the demands of human experience. In consequence, many important elements that belong to a holistic education, such as moral, spiritual and ecological formation through empathy, memory and imagination, are neglected or ignored.

The continuing strong presence of Christian inspiration in the conduct of our education system provides a basis for engaging with others who are concerned that our children should be supported to flourish across all the dimensions of life, and not shaped for a narrow role in the operation of the market economy.

The **ecological crisis** poses profound challenges for Ireland, in the areas of both economic production and consumption. The scale of some of the implicit changes required for sustainability deter many from engaging with the challenge. In some respects, the challenge is akin to personal conversion, with philosophical and moral dimensions, as well as behavioural change, involved. Discussion must therefore go beyond the crafting of specific public policy changes. The underlying call to respect nature and acknowledge the human impact on our world is one to which the Christian can bring a particularly creative perspective.

The overall health and dynamism of **civil society** is critical for the health of democracy. Voluntary effort and the non-profit sector challenge implicitly the dominant market forces of commercialisation and bureaucratisation. While proportionate and effective regulation is necessary if the confidence of donors and public bodies is to be retained, unsympathetic regulatory frameworks and overly commercial tendering practices by public bodies can stifle voluntary initiative and dull the communal capacity for creativity and innovation. The importance of voluntary action and advocacy in creating societal value and countering the narrow economising which may otherwise prevail needs to be acknowledged, and is an issue which merits wider debate than is provided by episodic focus on particular local failings.

Conclusion

The propositions set out in this Paper are a response to the widespread unease at clearly emerging trends in Irish society. They are a cause for particular unease for those who cherish the Christian vision of human development and social flourishing. There is a need and an opportunity to contribute to the evolution of debate, policy and practice in Ireland, and to forge alliances with those who share those concerns and aspirations. These include many who have drifted away from religious faith and practice, but who are still attracted by the values that frame the Christian vision of the good life, as well as many others with a committed and well-developed social philosophy grounded in their atheism and agnosticism. Patrick Hannon (2016) has observed that many conscientious people outside the faith share the Christian commitment to the dignity and equality of each human being, the rights that each possesses by virtue simply of being human, and all that is comprised in the concept of the common good. The decline in the institutional power of the Churches may enable them to contribute to civic dialogue more effectively out of this shared and now somewhat subversive value stance.

At any time, the civic republican vision for a flourishing society is inspired by the inherent human potential to learn and exercise collective power to build the world anew. A Christian may well see in this vision something of the 'abundant life' which Jesus Christ promises in his Kingdom of Love (*Jn 10:10*).

At this moment in Irish history, the needs of our people require a two-fold engagement, as articulated by Archbishop Diarmuid Martin (2016b). On the one hand,

> Ireland needs to overcome the intolerance of religion which can be found at times in an intransigent secularism which still feels that nothing can come from faith in that Jesus who 'was born in that place', a place which they consider alien.

But also, he believes,

> It is time for a Church to be present in society in such a way as to help people find that God revealed in Jesus Christ, not as an imposition but as an invitation to fullness of life.

This Paper is an appeal for all who share this deep unease at the conditions and trends revealed by the signs of our times to come forward and to engage in an enterprise of renewal. In challenging the conventional wisdom, this 'coalition of the willing' can become a 'coalition of hope', champions of a vision of a society where all can flourish and feel at home.

PART 2

FACING THE CHALLENGE

RELIGIOUS PERSPECTIVES AND THE PUBLIC SPHERE

ISEULT HONOHAN

Introduction

The current crisis of economy, politics and environment has driven us to reconsider the frames of reference we have taken for granted. The apparent failure of dominant ideologies, and the shortcomings of our economic and political frameworks in providing pointers to how we can live together and with what priorities, have brought about a sense of loss of direction, and the need to reach deeper to address our current predicament.

In the context of this loss of direction, it has been suggested that there are resources in religion and religious traditions from which we can learn by engaging with them (Habermas 2006). These traditions have been the concentrated locus of reflection on some of the deepest questions arising in human experience: the meaning of human life in the face of mortality, the possibility of transformation and transcendence, the freedom of individuals, solidarity among human beings, and their place in the larger picture of nature and the cosmos. Reflection on such questions may not be the exclusive preserve of religions, but they have long-standing experience and traditions in which responses to such deeper kinds of question were central.

The kinds of resources in religious traditions that come to mind here include: an openness to goods beyond the individual self, running counter to an individualist preoccupation and embracing wider relationships in community and in solidarity; a relative detachment from the worldly that runs counter to the consumerist approach to the world; and a situating of both self and society in a larger frame of existence that runs counter to the dominating or extractive approach to nature.

Whether we agree or not that religious perspectives have anything to contribute to our current concerns, however, it must first be considered whether it can be legitimate to bring religious viewpoints into the public realm in contemporary politics and society.

The Secular State

From one perspective, it seems that it can never be legitimate to bring religious viewpoints into the public realm, as this risks religious domination of the state, state domination of religious citizens, or destructive conflict between religions. This is why a secular state is needed.

There are different accounts of what secularism requires, however. We live in a continuing diversity of moral and religious perspectives, and an increasing pluralism of religions within and across states. The propensity of religious differences to cause conflict, and the way in which religious thinking appears unamenable to rational discussion, have indeed been significant concerns underpinning the movement towards political secularisation - the institutional separation of state and religion.*

The essential features of this separation are that the state itself does not impose any particular religion, and that it does not control religious groups. These features are sometimes referred to as the two freedoms of religion - freedom from religion, and freedom of religion. What is important is to limit the potential for the domination of citizens, whether by the state or by organised religions. There are differing views on other implications of secularism, of course: whether or not the state may provide any support or recognition for religious groups, and whether or not religious beliefs and practices must be excluded from the larger public sphere.

On one prominent view, different religions are tolerated and respected in private, but the State should not endorse them in any way, and the wider public sphere should be strictly neutral with respect to religion. This implies the exclusion of public expressions of religious belief. This version of secularism is endorsed most clearly by the French Republic in its doctrine of *laïcité*.

Secularism as it exists today, however, emerged historically from the evolution of the particular relationships between the State and Christianity in modern Europe, in which control by the State was the issue. More broadly, it has been pointed out that, because of its historical origins, the predominant modern model of secularism is a reversal or mirror-image of the earlier identification of Church and State: where previously religion was imposed by the State, it is now to be excluded from the State.

---

* Two senses of secularisation are sometimes confounded: the increasing separation of Church and State power, and the waning of religious belief. The former is not dependent on the latter, however. Indeed, the theory that religion is on the wane, in terms of numbers of believers and the social salience of religion, is not borne out globally (Casanova 1994).

There is in fact no single universal formula for the institutional provisions needed to avoid the threat of domination posed by the connection of political power and religion. The forms that the secular state has taken are various, reflecting their historical contexts, with different institutional arrangements for the relationship of religion to the public realm. Even in states that adopt principles of strict separation between the state and religion, as in France and the USA, different practices have emerged; one excludes all reference to religion in public, whereas the other allows freedom of individual religious expression and accommodates religious minorities in a range of ways. In the USA, it has been argued, 'separation was designed to free religion from state interference, whereas in France separation has evolved to exclude religion from public space and to promote the supremacy of the state over religious organisations' (Olivier Roy, cited in Chassany 2016). In practice, aspects of traditionally powerful religions are still embodied in both societies. For example, France funds religious – predominantly Catholic – schools; in the USA, God is invoked in the Pledge of Allegiance. In other western democracies, other solutions have evolved, which separate State and Church more and less strictly in realising the two underlying objectives, freedom from and of religion.

A more fundamental problem arises with approaches that favour the strict exclusion of religious expression in public. It is the danger of eliding two senses of the public sphere: the authoritative decision-making institutions of the State, and the wider space of discourse and deliberation. To separate religion from the exercise of public power does not necessarily require excluding it from public expression and discussion.

For these kinds of reasons, it has been argued that what political secularism should mean today needs further consideration if it is to allow for both freedom of the State from religious control, and freedom of religious citizens from domination by the State (Calhoun et al. 2011; Cohen and Laborde 2015; Laborde 2017a & b).

Why Religious Expressions Should Not Be Excluded from the Public Sphere

In this paper, I aim to outline why, even while we guard against the use of State power over or by religions, religious expression should not be excluded from the broader public realm and public deliberation. I will deal with three kinds of consideration: justice to religious citizens; practical political integration of minorities; and the possibility of mutual learning in deliberation on the common good in society among different moral and religious perspectives.

Reasons of Justice

A blanket privatising strategy with respect to religion can be seen as imposing different costs on members of different religions. Such a strategy affects less those whose religion is centred on belief and conscience, or whose practices fit more easily into the distinction between private and public, than those whose religion is more focused on ritual and practice. Members of religious minorities who have to choose, for example, between following religious practices or participating in education, employment or public service may be seen as dominated by the state that imposes this conditionality. Think, for instance, of Muslim girls or Sikh boys in France, who cannot attend public schools while wearing religious headwear; or the Sikh trainee who was not allowed to wear a turban in the Garda Reserve in Ireland. It may also be argued that if expressions of citizens' deepest convictions are restricted to the private realm, this downgrades their significance, and fails to treat them as equal citizens. If, further, political arguments based on religious reasoning are disallowed in the political realm, this reinforces any majority bias in the status quo, and remains an exercise of power in which religious citizens – especially those belonging to a minority – are at a disadvantage.

To be treated equally, citizens need an equal legal and political status, in which they are protected by the rule of law, and can express a voice in political deliberation. Equal citizenship among diverse citizens is realised, not by excluding religion from the public realm, but by even-handedly accommodating non-dominating practices of religious – and non-religious – citizens, and by allowing them to express their perspectives in the public realm of deliberation. If there are some particular roles in which strict neutrality is essential, this should apply equally to all, and with consideration of the impact for the equality of minorities in society. It is also necessary to be continually open to consider and to change ways in which existing arrangements in the State may dominate citizens of diverse beliefs (Carens 2000).

In response to the objection that this facilitates domination within religious groups, particularly of women, it can be replied that if we are concerned to reduce domination, the state should indeed be alert to the threat of oppression, and intervene to constrain dominating practices. As John Maynor puts it, individuals and groups within a republican state can be non-liberals, but they cannot be dominators (2003). While this will have clear implications with respect to some practices, the interpretation of wearing headscarves is notoriously contested in this regard. For some, the practice suggests clearly a domination over women; for some wearers, it is an autonomous expression of a distinct identity, or a political gesture.

Thus, Cécile Laborde's 'critical republicanism', in the interests of the republican values of freedom and equality, argues for greater neutrality of political institutions than in France at present, with fewer constraints on the expression of religious minorities, rather than strict exclusion of religious expressions (2008).

Reasons of Integration

More pragmatic considerations for the support of democratic society also favour greater public accommodation of religious beliefs and practices, especially in the case of minorities.

It has been argued that the danger of alienation from a society in which religion is confined to the private sphere may be overcome, for example, by accommodating religious practices, and drawing religious minorities into society through institutional provisions for representing and including them in deliberation and compromises. Such accommodation may increase their willingness to integrate in and trust liberal democratic political systems. Veit Bader, on the basis of a conception of justice as even-handedness, in contrast to justice as neutrality, has argued, for example, that, among other political and institutional accommodations of religious diversity, a state-supported and state-regulated pluralist system of schools is more appropriate than either a wholly secular system based on the idea of neutrality or the absolute accommodation of religious groups in education (2007). This entails requiring a core curriculum, equal opportunities for girls and boys, and inspection of schools, alongside a range of more pragmatic accommodations. This approach acknowledges that every system of education strikes a particular balance between, on the one hand, individual religious liberty and non-discrimination, and, on the other hand, collective religious freedom, while catering for other concerns, such as social cohesion and the need for civic education, as well. Which of these concerns are most salient will vary with different social and political contexts, and different ways of striking the balance may be appropriate in different contexts.

It is difficult to identify any state that has systematically pursued policies of the kind recommended by Bader, though the UK has been seen as adopting something like this approach to incorporating religious minorities. In Ireland, a system of institutional pluralism in education in particular gave religious groups the right to have their own schools with state support, but leaned more towards collective than individual religious freedom, and in practice was predominantly Catholic. The system may now be evolving towards greater pluralism along Bader's lines, rather than either secularisation or absolute accommodation of religious groups (Rougier and Honohan 2015).

By contrast to this kind of accommodation, Bader claims that policies 'to enforce assimilation on dominant ethno-religious cultures (masked as "secular", "neutral" or "purely civic") by legal and other sanctions are most likely to provoke reactive ethnicisation, religious fundamentalism and radical communal organisation, mobilisation and conflict if minorities command sufficient resources to resist' (Bader 2007). (See also Walzer 2015.)

In France, which has adopted what Laborde terms 'a

tough-minded version of egalitarian, difference-blind liberalism', the refusal of the state to acknowledge religious diversity
has not prevented (and in some respects may have contributed
to) increasing inequality, educational and housing segregation and
disaffection among some Muslims (Laborde 2008).

Reasons of Mutual Learning

Engagement between different religious and non-religious perspectives may be able to cast light on the social and political issues
that concern us now.

Religious perspectives have often been central to social and political change. Consider, for example, Quaker leadership in the
movement against slavery in the eighteenth century; Gandhi's
inspiration for non-violence in Buddhism, Hinduism and Jain-
ism; the evangelical Protestant emphasis underlying Martin Lu-
ther King's campaign for civil rights; liberation theology's role in
supporting movements for democracy in Latin America; and the
role of forgiveness and the possibility of personal redemption in
South Africa's Truth and Reconciliation Commission and in the
Northern Ireland peace process.

Among key aspects of these movements was the way in which
they made aspects of the harms that they challenged and the com-
pelling vision that underpinned their causes salient and conspicu-
ous. Even if similar ideas were latent in enlightenment, liberal and
democratic thinking, it was when articulated in language that drew
on religious perspectives that they gained real purchase. Thus, it
can be argued that conceptions of individual human dignity and
communal solidarity, if not originating in religious perspectives,
have been significantly influenced by them.

In promoting social and political reform, of course, religious contributions have not always been dialogic, but have often been dogmatic in approach. On this basis, some argue that religions are ill-suited for dialogue and deliberative exchange. Religions make specific truth-claims that are central to their beliefs. They cannot be expected to set them aside. They can, however, be expected to set aside claims to impose them on others without their assent. As Maeve Cooke notes (2006, 2007), we should distinguish between religious claims and authoritarian claims; it is not religious discourse that is problematic but authoritarian discourse, and it can appear in religious or secular forms. There are deliberative, as well as authoritarian traditions, within many religions (Sen 2009). This may not be true of all religions to the same extent, and even where deliberative strands are present, these may need to be further drawn out, especially with respect to gender.

Even if not dogmatic or authoritarian in their approach to deliberation, religious views, as well as other comprehensive moral views, involve commitments to certain fundamental beliefs that are not always reconcilable. Thus dialogue may often clarify disagreements rather than lead to agreement. It may be argued that encouraging public discussion between such perspectives risks outright conflict. We have seen, however, that excluding religious discussion in public itself has not prevented the build-up of hostility and conflict from those whose perspectives are marginalised.

It is true that comprehensive agreement on fundamental beliefs will be unlikely to emerge from dialogue. But the achievement of consensus is not the only valuable goal of such exchanges. If they are prepared to listen as well as speak, people on both sides of the exchange may become more aware of the specificity and limitations of their own positions, or the extent to which they follow them through in practice or fail to do so. They may come to understand the other better, and the way in which their vision of the good underpins their beliefs and practices. This is less likely when religious arguments are excluded from public debate, or when religious citizens may either abstain from debate, or try to express their views in constructed 'secular' formulations.

There may also be times when one or both parties come to see the implications of their beliefs differently as a result of the exchange. Given the limits of argument, we may want to think about this less as a matter of rational argumentation than an experience of shifting of horizons, a new way of seeing things when we consider the other's point of view. As Cooke (2013) puts it,

> When it comes to questions of the good life and good society, in many cases we will fail to be convinced by the arguments of others until we have undergone ... [a] significant shift in perception. Such shifts in perception involve truth as disclosure, whereby the world, or some aspect of it, appears in a different light and we gain a new way of looking at things. While the required shift in perception may be brought about argumentatively, as when we are swayed by the arguments of others, it typically depends on non-argumentative experiences, which make us receptive to these arguments or, indeed, substitute for them.

As noted earlier, it was in part the vivid articulation of their vision of the good that made religious interventions for social change so powerful. Religious views of individual human dignity, duties

of solidarity and responsibility for the environment may offer resources now when these appear to be marginalised. Even those
who acknowledge their importance have difficulty working out
how to articulate or realise them in the new economic and political circumstances. What does respect for individual dignity and
duties of solidarity mean under the market-determined conditions of family life, work and consumption in contemporary global society? What do they mean for those who are vulnerable in
society? What does solidarity mean for immigrants and refugees
and the global distant poor, when national boundaries appear to
be hardening again? How can responsibility for the environment
be recognised and acted upon?

These are concerns for religious and non-religious people alike;
whatever their differences, they face a common future in an increasingly interdependent world and a threatened natural environment. As interdependent citizens, they need to deliberate on
what constitutes the common good in these circumstances. The
common good cannot be determined from a single perspective,
but involves reflecting on, rather than bracketing, different fundamental beliefs. Religious expressions on these matters can be ar-
resting when articulated against a background where their secular
counterparts may seem to have lost their motivating force.

Conclusion

The importance of a secular state, in which religious and political
power are separate, can be recognised without implying that there
is no place for religious ideas and discourse in public discussion.
We have seen, on both justice and integration grounds, that religion should not be excluded from the public realm. Moreover,

democratic political renewal may be inspired by religious ideas and commitments. Accordingly, we should not rule out the possibility that new ways of addressing the concerns outlined in some of the other chapters here may be inspired by religious approaches. Neither should we dismiss the value of dialogue between religious and non-religious views in providing hope in a social, economic and political world where conventional approaches have worn thin. Bringing together religious and secular perspectives may offer a way to focus on questions that fall through the cracks of market discourse. Whether and how humans can continue to inhabit the planet; how the economy might be made to work for all; how inequality and poverty can be addressed; how the vulnerable can be protected; whether solidarity operates within borders or globally across them: these are questions to which we need to develop alternative visions and approaches, in the absence of which their significance risks being, if not denied, overlooked.

KEY AREAS FOR CONSTRUCTIVE ENGAGEMENT: SOLIDARITY, COMMUNITY AND ACTIVE CITIZENSHIP

FERGUS O'FERRALL

The age of party democracy has passed. Although the parties themselves remain, they have become so disconnected from the wider society, and pursue a form of competition that is so lacking in meaning, that they no longer seem capable of sustaining democracy in its present form.

Peter Mair (2013)

Introduction – Let's Be Clear What We Are Talking about!
A 'dialogue of hope' between Christians and those of other faiths and of none will find much common ground in a new project to promote human flourishing. Together, such a coalition might tell an alternative story about how we may flourish together. As Ivan Illich (1926-2002), philosopher and priest, has reminded us:

Neither revolution nor reformation can ultimately change a society, rather you must tell a new powerful tale, one so persuasive that it sweeps away the old

49

myths and becomes the preferred story, one so inclusive that it gathers all the bits of our past and our present into a coherent whole, one that even shines some light on the future so that we can take the next step ... If you want to change a society, then you have to tell an alternative story (Buzzard 2013, citing Illich).

The alternative story we might tell together is one where we share fundamental concepts about human dignity and rights, the search for the common good, and about our duties and responsibilities to other human beings in solidarity, community and as active citizens in a new civic republic.

A flourishing human society will be characterised by solidarity, community and active citizenship. In the midst of the great crisis of the American Civil War, Abraham Lincoln delivered his famous Gettysburg Address on 19 November 1863. As we confront our multi-faceted crisis we need to hear his words afresh. Lincoln's call is for living citizens to be dedicated to 'unfinished work ... the great task remaining before us ... that this nation, under God, shall have a new birth of freedom – and that government of the people, by the people, for the people shall not perish from the earth'.

Lincoln fought a bloody civil war so that the great experiment of representative democracy in the nineteenth century might succeed. Representative democracy is now in crisis. Our 'new birth of freedom' in the twenty-first century must involve rescuing representative government through the experiment of participatory democracy. We must build a citizen society. We must nurture old and new seedbeds of the civic virtues where solidarity, community and active citizenship develop and are experienced. These seedbeds lie in civil society, voluntary organisations and in faith communities. They might also be in schools, if education were to become for students a genuine democratic and participatory experience.

What do we mean by solidarity, community and active citizenship? About them there appears to be a depth of civic ignorance, and our first task is to address such deficits by having clarity about what they mean.

Solidarity

Lip service is often paid to 'solidarity'. For example, solidarity is one of the six principles of the Charter of Fundamental Rights of the European Union, and Human Solidarity Day is celebrated each year on 20 December. Solidarity is unity amongst citizens, a unity of empathy and action concerning the common good, which involves mutual support given to each person or group according to need. The poet Oliver Goldsmith wrote of 'ties that bind and sweeten life'; such ties are based upon the dignity, equality and sacredness of each human person.

In ethical discourse, solidarity is discussed at three levels as it is enacted at the inter-personal, the communal and the legal levels. In respect of building a flourishing society that facilitates others in living full lives, it is social solidarity that is crucial. This means developing in citizens the knowledge, skills and attitudes that equip them to behave in relation to other people as they would wish others to treat them. We should not be reluctant to claim the faith perspective that calls on us to love our neighbours as ourselves.

Community

This is where the concept of community becomes central. Community is a term that is frequently used loosely of any collection of individuals. If, however, we are going to use the word to mean a flourishing human society – a political community – then we must restrict it to citizens who have learned how to communicate honestly with each other, who have demonstrated empathy for other people, and who have developed a significant commitment to action for their mutual welfare. Inclusivity, commitment and consensus are the marks of a political community that promotes human flourishing for all its members. The great enemy of community is exclusivity. Groups that exclude others on social, ethnic, sexual, religious or nationality grounds are not healthy political groups.

Hence the willingness to coexist in all our human variety and a commitment to this are crucial to our well-being as we learn to transcend individual differences and rejoice in diversity as gifts to human flourishing. This commitment goes well beyond a representative democratic order in which the majority rules. Rather, it seeks to create a participatory democratic order, in which all minorities have creative and full engagement. The approach to decision-making is in favour of consensus at all levels. These marks of healthy political communities which display strong social solidarity require the virtues we develop as active citizens.

Active Citizenship

The term 'active citizen' stems from a political philosophy which is called 'civic republicanism' (Pettit 1997, 2014; Honohan 2002). This philosophy doesn't see citizenship only as a status entitling a

person to formal rights enshrined in law. Civic republicanism emphasises the civic virtues of participation, social solidarity, freedom as non-domination, equality and the collective pursuit of the
common good. A civic republic characterised by active citizens
is an achieved political community which promotes, in Lincoln's
words, a 'new birth of freedom' and 'government of the people,
by the people, for the people'. Active citizenship, characterised by
the required civic virtues, is a learned phenomenon and requires
a range of preconditions for development (Bellamy 2008; Crick
2000; Crick and Lockyer 2010).

Thinking Big in Dark Times

Where do we learn virtues, like an awareness of our interdependence, empathy and an attitude of self-restraint, in order to
achieve the common good and an openness to deliberative engagement and the skills of participation? The cultural transmis-
sion of norms, ideas and practices is a complex process. This
may be seen from the story of democratic development in our
own country from Daniel O'Connell's birthing of Irish democratic politics in the 1820s and the subsequent evolution of our
political culture.

Today, if we are to develop a civic republic shaped by solidarity, community and active citizenship, as outlined above, we must
start from where we are in Ireland now, in this decade of cente-
naries. In the course of these years – 2012-2022 – we are invited
to reflect upon our past, of course, but also importantly to re-
imagine our future. We must think afresh and think big, even as
the western world has plunged into a dark time for democratic
politics. When those of faith and those of no faith work together

in the public square, then opportunities in their deliberations to think big must arise.

Thinking anew and thinking big is now imperative, given the democratic crisis in the Western world. As Hannah Arendt, the political philosopher, has taught us, there is a fundamental relationship between thinking correctly and our right-doing and, conversely, between our thoughtlessness – or indeed our 'captive' minds – and wrong-doing (Berkowitz et al. 2010).

The capacity to think is inherent in the human person, but it must be nurtured. We need to develop opportunities for fresh thinking by all citizens if we are to be free of failed conventional ideologies or of unexamined prejudices or beliefs. Arendt's work reminds us that in 'dark times, thinking brings much-needed light and clarity'. We should not be afraid to reimagine together the whole Irish republican democratic project. Achieving a truly Irish civic republic shaped by solidarity, community and active citizenship will demand no less.

What Is To Be Done? Possible Lines of Action

Reimagining a very different kind of Republic – one closer to genuine republican philosophy, as understood down the centuries – requires a major paradigm shift in public consciousness. What is to be done to facilitate such a shift?

Deliberative Processes: a Network of Civic Fora

Innovative, open, cooperative, inclusive and continuous public deliberative processes are essential to the renewal of progressive politics and to the defining and sharing of a civic republican vision. There are already some successful examples of such processes at work in Ireland at national and local levels, such as the ethics initiative of President Michael D. Higgins, the Constitutional Convention, the Citizens Assembly, The People's Conversation, TASC, Second Republic, People Talk and the all-island Civic Dialogue on Brexit. There are others at local and national levels that could be named as well. All of these have served in different ways to facilitate citizens themselves in shaping our future, rather than simply enduring it.

To build on these innovative initiatives, and to facilitate more widespread participation alongside a truly reformed representative local government system, I suggest that a key priority should be the development of a new citizen-based Civic Forum in each county and city in Ireland. The ideal of government of the people, by the people, for the people points to a participatory democracy which does not exclude the people from self-government, as our current structures do, and does not alienate them from the political system, as the clientelism of our representative system does at present. The experiments carried out so far, such as the Constitutional Convention and the Citizens Assembly, indicate that innovation is possible. Civic fora would provide vital public spaces and public deliberative opportunities to bring thousands more into public life. In this regard, there are important lessons to be learned from Scotland, where public deliberation was institutionalised in governance since devolution (Davidson and Stark 2011). In particular, lessons might be learned concerning the use of committees and deliberative processes within a national legislature, and how public engagement can be promoted at local-authority levels. For example, the use of 'public engagers' to develop a new politics of process, as employed in Scotland, might be considered. This is not the place to evaluate in detail what might be learned and adopted in the Republic, but such learning ought to be added to our list to tasks to be done as we plan new deliberative processes.

Tooling up: Developing Together New Conceptual Tools

In order to live in a flourishing society oriented around the common good and characterised by solidarity, community and active citizenship, citizens need to be equipped with the necessary conceptual tools. For example, how do we collectively define 'growth'? Is it by Gross Domestic Product or do we employ more meaningful well-being measures? Do ordinary citizens understand what the concept of 'sustainable development' involves? In an age of inequality, have citizens understood how the ideology which they have so generally embraced has allowed massive inequalities to emerge? Have the widespread negative effects of such inequalities – not least the erosion of representative democracy in so many countries – been widely understood? If the environment is to be protected from human-induced degradation, has public understanding of, and support for, socially inclusive and environmentally sustainable growth been developed? Surely such support will require that the concepts embedded in these phrases are widely understood.

A whole battery of new opportunities needs to be realised to allow active citizens to develop the conceptual tools required to build a flourishing human society and to facilitate critical thinking in a digital age. Naturally, one looks to educational institutions to develop such conceptual and critical thinking – and the moves to teach philosophy in schools may be lauded in this context – but the challenge is also a critical one for adult and community education. A radical new approach to adult education must accompany the paradigm shift required. Historically, the contribution of the folk high schools in Scandinavian countries, inspired by N. F. S. Grundtvig in the late nineteenth century, provides one illustration of the levels of adult education and of the kind of transformative cultural shift now demanded if we are seeking to develop a flourishing society (Thaning 1972; Allchin 1997).

Organise, Organise and then Reorganise! Models for the Public Square

Collective action by citizens is of paramount importance, and is required at local, national and transnational levels. The creation of a republican political community based upon equality, liberty and solidarity depends on active citizens working towards common goals.

The creation of such a community will require a new balance between, on the one hand, the need for progressive political party organisations to build a stronger capacity to define political programmes, plans or positions, and, on the other hand, the necessity of guaranteeing that these are the result of continuous, inclusive and participatory processes. Party organisations, while retaining their role of integrating citizen concerns into coherent political programmes, need to evolve into networked exchanges, permanently providing multiple, open and easy-to-access channels in which citizens and civil society can engage, contribute and mobilise around causes and concerns. The network of new civic fora, proposed above, would provide a necessary but not sufficient condition for this enrichment of the party political system. For a new age of participatory democracy to be sufficiently robust to prevent authoritarian movements gaining power in our enfeebled representative systems, a new and permanent connection between progressive political organisations, progressive civil society and active citizens at all levels is required.

Truth-telling and giving public witness about our common values – often through public protests and proclamation – will become ever more important in the age of far-right propaganda, the denigration of a free and independent news media, and 'alternative facts'. As Garry Kasparov, the Russian dissenter and chess grandmaster, has said, speaking from his experience of Putinesque authoritarianism, 'The point of modern propaganda isn't only to misinform or push an agenda. It is to exhaust your critical thinking, to annihilate truth'.

Politics can never be allowed to become divorced from truth. For Christians, Jesus is the Way, The Truth and the Life and, in acknowledging him and not Caesar as Lord, they should have an in-built protection from deference to any human leaders, particularly political leaders and systems of a totalitarian tendency. Christians are called to witness to this in the public square and bring the courage of their convictions as a gift to everyone in society. It is time for Christian Churches to rethink fundamentally how they ought to witness to the gospel in the public square and how they might listen to secular society in order to 'read the signs of the times'. The common good is served neither by a theocratic model of 'the one true faith' – whether Islamic or Christian – imposed exclusively on public laws, nor by a 'naked public square' model which excludes religious or faith-based contributions. What is now required is a 'civic public square' model which rejects both the privatisation of faith and the politicisation of faith. This model involves a vision of public life in which citizens of all faiths are free to enter and engage the public square on the basis of their faith, within a republican constitutional and legal framework, where all citizens, secular and religious, are equal and are required to give public reasons for whatever they advocate in the interests of the common good (O'Ferrall 2014).

New Measures of Well-being

'It's the economy, stupid!' was a famous phrase of the neo-liberal era, meaning that political choices at the end of the day are determined by those who can manage to 'grow' the economy best. Now, as we move beyond GDP as the measure of success, the catchphrase we need might well become, 'It's about quality of life for all, stupid!' We have seen high GDP growth rates in the past leaving vast numbers in poverty – as in the USA – and too many without access to basic services such as health, education or welfare. These inequalities have given rise to anti-democratic movements exploiting the insecurities and fears of those sections of the populations who have lost work and incomes as well as hope for the future. To ensure all citizens may have flourishing lives, a civic republic must guarantee that the wealth and income of our society will be deployed to provide *universal public services in health, education (including higher education) and welfare (including a floor of welfare or basic income for every citizen)*. These universal public services will be paid for collectively by all citizens through progressive taxation of wealth and income. We owe each other no less if we see each other as equal citizens in a republic. This is where solidarity is best tested and realised. This is an essential basis for a flourishing human society (Reynolds and Healy 2015).

Two relatively recent publications are worthy of note in the present context. The OECD developed in 2013 its *Framework for Measuring Well-Being and Progress*, based upon the recommendations made in 2009 by the Commission on the Measurement of Economic Performance and Social Progress. The National Economic and Social Council issued in 2009 a Report entitled *Well-being Matters, A Social Report*, and proposed a 'well-being test' which ought to be key in relation to public policy development.

Conclusion

Michael Sandel, the political philosopher, has argued persuasively (2009, 2012) that social justice involves cultivating virtue and public reasoning about the common good:

> A just society can't be achieved simply by maximising utility or by securing freedom of choice. To achieve a just society we have to reason together about the meaning of the good life, and to create a public culture hospitable to the disagreements that will inevitably arise ... The challenge is to imagine a politics that takes moral and spiritual questions seriously, but brings them to bear on broad economic and civic concerns, not only on sex and abortion.

Deep and widespread public deliberation should be accorded to Sandel's framework of key themes for 'a new politics of the common good': citizenship, sacrifice and service, the moral limits of markets, inequality, solidarity, and civic virtue; and a politics of moral engagement.

It is worth noting that a Task Force on Active Citizenship, set up by the Irish Government in 2006, had this to say in the – largely ignored – report it subsequently produced (2007):

> [Without] the practice of civic virtue and without active participation by citizens in the life of the community, the institutions of democracy, the market, the State-civil society as a whole- cannot operate in a sustainable way.

The late Peter Mair, one of Ireland's leading political scientists, stated trenchantly (2011) that Ireland has a 'moribund politics and a moribund political culture.' We have at present an Irish polity in which our people are, in Mair's words, both 'demobilised as well as demoralised'. We have, he believed, a disengaged and passive citizenry, an ineffective political class, and a political world which has ceded much of its control to other organisations and groups, and which has become autonomous and self-contained, rarely connecting in any meaningful sense to life outside itself. Politics in these circumstances becomes an end in itself, and becomes a contest that is played out for its own benefit and that of its players. It is not something that requires engagement with or mobilisation of the citizenry at large – that happens at a much more personalistic and local level by the parish pump – and hence it encourages passivity.

Mair's analysis is one we ignore at our peril.

In reimaging a new Civic Republic in Ireland, we face an enormous and long-term challenge. However, the potential of people to renew their world – in Thomas Paine's words 'We can make the world anew' – is evident from history. Elsewhere, I have written:

> The new Civic Republic of Ireland will, I believe,
> stand for a great and generous experiment in human
> well-being and happiness. It will be founded upon an

educated and intellectually vibrant citizenry, imbued with the civic virtues and dedicated to the common good. It will develop a society where every person will be enabled to exercise the whole range of their human capacities and live rewarding and fulfilling lives as part of an energetic and humane political community (O'Ferrall 2012).

ANTHROPOLOGY IN THE SERVICE OF BRIDGES TO HOPE

DERMOT A. LANE

Introduction

In the opening paper by Dermot McCarthy to this collection of essays, 'Signs of our Times', there is a recognition that anthropology is a factor underlying much of the social, political and economic malaise of modern Ireland. Anthropology is the study of what it means to be a human being, an examination of what is at the core of human identity, an analysis of what promotes human flourishing, and an exploration of human nature in the light of the social sciences, history, philosophy and theology. The surest sign of a deep crisis in anthropology is our contemporary inability to talk seriously about death in the public forum.

The aim of this paper is to construct an anthropology that builds bridges between human beings, that paves the way for a new dialogue between secularists and believers, and that facilitates the formation of a coalition of hope among people of secular and theistic convictions. The paper will seek to do this in four steps.

Part One will show that anthropology is in crisis in a number of different disciplines. Part Two will outline some of the elements that could contribute to a reconstruction of anthropology in the twenty-first century. Part Three will show how a renewed anthropology could build bridges for a coalition of hope among secularists and believers. Part Four will conclude with a brief introduction to the shape of a theology of hope within this coalition.

Anthropology – a Contested Area

Anthropology is a red thread running through many areas of life: ecology, economics, ethics, education, philosophy and theology.

On ecology, Pope Francis and the UN Conference on Climate Change in Paris both agreed in 2015 with the scientific view that the ecological crisis is caused mostly by human activity and certain expressions of anthropocentrism. Pope Francis (2015a) is explicit in his criticism of what he calls 'tyrannical', 'distorted', 'excessive' and 'misguided' forms of anthropocentrism. Further, he points out that there can be no ecology without an adequate anthropology.

In economics, Jeffrey Sachs (2016), US economist and UN adviser, gave a keynote address on 'Economics for the Common Good' to a conference in the London School of Economics in December 2016. In his opening words, he pointed out that 'Economics went wildly off-track by a profoundly flawed model of human nature and a flawed model of human purpose'.

In the area of ethics, the President of Ireland, Michael D. Higgins, has sought to open a national debate. In an address entitled 'Toward an Ethical Economy' (2013), given in DCU as part of a series on 'Ethics for All', he has argued that a 'culture devoid of ethics, in many of our institutions, has played a key role in our nation's loss of prosperity and economic sovereignty'. Part of the problem, the President has said elsewhere (2015), has been the rise of 'extreme individualism, grounded in a hegemonic version of the market without limit'. Further, the failure to 'question the concept of individualism and insatiable consumption' has been a contributing factor to our recent economic crisis.

In the field of education, there is concern about the increasing influence of technology, metrics and managerialism at all levels of education in Ireland. Too much emphasis is placed on production, where outcomes are prescribed in advance of the learning experience. Part of the problem with this approach to education is the presence of an anthropological reductionism, which neglects areas such as the holistic development of students, inter-personal skills, collaboration, leadership, empathetic memory and the exercise of the creative imagination. Genuine education, according to Michael Kirwan (2017), is about the search for wisdom, and not just information and knowledge. It should go beyond a mechanistic scientism of the person, in which the human vanishes and the art of living the good life is lost.

In philosophy, both modern and post-modern, anthropology has been, and continues to be, deeply debated. Modern philosophy has been marked by a turn to the subject, and this has resulted in the emergence of the sovereign subject of modernity. The separated self was, and is, so strong, so confident and so independent that it has become the ground of its own being: self-sufficient, self-defining and self-sustaining, without reference to any reality outside itself.

By way of reaction, post-modern philosophy radically deconstructs the self-sufficient subject of modernity. This programme of deconstruction can be summed up in the words of Michel Foucault (1970): 'Man is an invention of recent date' and will be 'erased like a face drawn in the sand at the edge of the sea'. For some post-moderns, the self is just a rhetorical flourish, a linguistic and cultural construct to facilitate the interaction of differences.

Within Catholic feminist theology, there is a storm stirring around anthropology in relation to identity, sexuality and gender, and how these impact on the role of women in the life of the Church. Recent Popes, especially John Paul II, have presented an anthropology of men and women as essentially different but complementary - as complete, not in themselves, but only in relation to each other. This particular anthropology has handicapped the participation of the Catholic Church in public debates concerning marriage equality, ecclesial governance and ministry. The experience and praxis of women, as well as the impact of the Christ event on human identity in the New Testament (e.g. *Gal 3:28; 5:6; 6:15; 2 Cor 5:17*), needs to inform this debate.

Restructuring Anthropologies for the Twenty-first Century
Given the problems around anthropology in the above areas, it is clear that some reconstruction of anthropology is necessary for the twenty-first century. In restructuring what it means to be human, we must move beyond the modern idea that one anthropology fits all. Some authors talk about multi-polar anthropologies, while others refer to the multidimensional character of human identity. There are, in truth, many different selves: the private and public self, the social and professional self, the secular and religious self. The human, therefore, is a multi-layered, finely

wrought work of art permanently in process. Equally, we must move beyond the atomised self – what Charles Taylor calls the 'buffered self' – of modern society.

In moving towards a multi-polar account of human identity, pride of place must be given to the dignity that belongs to every human being, a dignity that transcends race, sex, health and class. It is no accident that the language of human dignity came to the fore after the Second World War, as a reaction to the atrocities of that war and especially the Holocaust.

The concept of human dignity was written into the Charter of the United Nations in 1945, and given particular expression in the UN *Universal Declaration of Human Rights* in 1948. Human dignity is about the intrinsic value that belongs to every human being. People are born with this dignity, carry this dignity throughout life, and die with this dignity. This unique, universal dignity embraces respect for the freedom of the individual, for the rational and affective life of each person, and for the conscience of every human being.

Prior to the establishment of the United Nations, human dignity was seen as something grounded in the Judaeo-Christian tradition, especially in terms of the human as made in the image and likeness of God (*Gen 1:26*). Since the foundation of the United Nations, the dignity of human beings has been perceived as a concept available through the use of reason. Without neglecting the religious roots of human dignity in the monotheistic faith, this secular understanding of human dignity was recognised by Pope John XXIII in his encyclical *Pacem in Terris* (1963) and in particular, two years later, at the Second Vatican Council in the *Pastoral Constitution on the Church in the*

Modern World and in the *Decree on Religious Liberty*.

Closely related to this near-worldwide acceptance of human dignity, and complementary to it, is a recognition that the human is a radically relational reality. This relational dimension stands out in stark contrast to the individualism of the modern era. In reaction to Descartes's influential 'I think, therefore, I am', we must move towards an anthropology which recognises, first of all, that 'we are before I am' or, as an African proverb puts it, 'We relate, therefore, I am'. Pierre Teilhard de Chardin (1971), reflecting on evolution, observes that what comes first is not being but union, which gives rise to being. Being is first a 'we' before it can become an 'I'. To exist, therefore, is always to coexist; to be is to be in relationship; being (*esse*) is always being towards (*esse ad*).

Linked to this relational understanding of human identity is the discovery that it is only in the gift of self to others that we find out who we really are. Self-realisation comes about in the giving of oneself to the other. Self-surrender yields self-discovery. The human is at his or her best in the gift of self to the other. What begins to emerge within this focus on the relational and social self is that we do not come into the world with a ready-made self. We are not born with an 'I'; instead, we leave the world with an emerging self which exists as an unfinished project.

Flowing from this relational anthropology is the discovery of the importance of dialogue. It is in and through dialogue that the genesis, development and flourishing of human identity takes place. The human not only enters into dialogue with others, but it is in the dynamics of dialogue that there awakens within the self something that would otherwise remain dormant.

A further dimension to the complexity of the self is the importance of recognising that the self exists only as embodied. Human identity, human consciousness and interiority are only available as embodied. Neuro-science highlights the intimate relationship that exists between psychological phenomena and physical phenomena, between the activities of the self and the reactions of the brain. There is a sense in which human subjectivity is more than matter and yet it is only available in and through particular activities of the brain. This emphasis on embodiment invites a new respect for and valuation of the human body.

No account of anthropology would be complete without reference to the impact of cosmology, evolution and human development on our self-understanding. The new cosmologies and theories of evolution highlight the interdependent, interrelated and interconnected character of everything in the world. We live in a finely tuned universe, and this highlights the underlying unity of the cosmos, the earth and the human. Equally, it is now becoming frighteningly clear, in the light of the ecological crisis, that we interfere with this unity at our peril, and that this applies right across the spectrum of life, from the macrocosm of the universe to the microcosm of the human. Flowing from this is an awareness of the profound relationship that exists between humans and the earth. For example, many see the self as the earth in a state of self-consciousness and human freedom, with all the responsibility that flows from reflective self-consciousness and freedom for the well-being of the earth. The human is, in the words of Gerard Manley Hopkins (1918), 'earth's eye, tongue or heart' or, as Denise Levertov (1990) puts it, 'earth's mind, mirror, reflective source'.

Towards a Coalition of Hope

In the light of these multi-layered anthropologies, we can begin to explore the possibilities of a coalition of hope between secularists and believers.

It is often said that faith was the big question of the twentieth century: the possibility of faith in God in the face of so much suffering, tragedy and war. In the twenty-first century, it is hope that is becoming the big question in the face of so much apathy and indifference, so much cynicism and scepticism, so much failure and uncertainty. Within this new context, the possibility of forming a coalition of hope between secularists and believers, in the service of a more humane, more just and a more ecologically aware world, is urgent.

To open this conversation, I wish to distinguish between human hope and religious hope, even though they are closely related. Human hope is a this-worldly hope, and is inspired by attention to the dynamics of human experience, the movements of history and the needs of society. Religious hope is both a this-worldly hope *and* an other-worldly hope.

Further, it should be noted that 'I cannot hope alone'. It is possible, perhaps, to be optimistic alone, but hope is that which connects us to others, through the discovery that 'I cannot go it alone in this life'. In addition, hope, in contrast to optimism, is in short supply at present, partly because it has been supplanted by the modern myth of progress (optimism), partly because of the cultural denial of death, and partly because of the rise of a rugged individualism. And yet, it must be acknowledged that implicit and unspoken hopes exist in the lives of most people who just don't have the time or inclination to articulate them. A further introductory point about hope is that it is closely committed to praxis, that is to bringing about change and transformation within our own lives and that of society. I do what I hope and hope what I do.

Paul Ricoeur (1970) described hope as a protest against the premature closure of all systems of thought, especially religious and political fundamentalisms, as well as philosophical reductionisms and nihilisms. Hope keeps thought and action open and reacts against claims to absolute knowledge. Hope is an impulse that resists closure and refuses finality.

How then does hope get started? What is it that activates hope? To answer these questions, we must take a critical look at the dynamics of human experience. At some stage in life, we have 'contrast-experiences', that is experiences which point up a sharp contrast between what is and what could be. This occurs whenever there are violations of human dignity, when human rights are denied, when relationships break down, and when justice is trampled upon. Such experiences awaken a sense of indignation and outrage, a call to protest and action, a refusal to accept the status quo.

How do we move from 'contrast experiences' to hope? Part of the problem, historically speaking, is that we have become imprisoned in the practices of the past which rule the present. Western societies have been held captive to a market-driven capitalism and neo-liberal economics, where policies and decisions are measured according to the 'values' of the market and their support for the economy. Considerations about serving the dignity of the individual, the well-being of the human community and the earth-community, the integrity of human relationships and respect for human embodiment are of another order relative to the primacy of the market and dominance of the economy. And, yet, there is evidence that the reigning models of market-driven capitalism are not serving the well-being of communities, or the freedom of individuals, or the common goods of society and the environment.

No one has been more outspoken and prophetic in this regard than Pope Francis (2015b). He talks about an 'economy that kills' and berates those economic paradigms that promise more because they are premised on a lie which ignores that the resources of the earth are finite.

The dominance of the reigning models of capitalism and economics could be altered by a careful historical analysis of the social and political status quo. The role of the historian, according to the Frankfurt School of Critical Theory, is 'to brush history against the grain', so that the forgotten hopes of past generations can re-emerge in the present. Memory has the power to reopen history so as to allow the voices of the victims of history to speak in the present and ensure that the injustices of the past may not be repeated in the future. When this happens, as in many of the commissions concerned with truth and reconciliation around the world, the grip of the past on the present can be broken open, and the possibility of hope in the present can begin to emerge. Without this possibility, history appears as a vicious circle, giving rise to more of the same, producing pessimism, cynicism and fatalism. For this power of memory to reopen the past in the present, there must be empathy with the victims of history.

This power of empathetic memory to generate hope in the present will only succeed to the extent that it is linked to imagination, not just to revisit the past but, more importantly, to offer alternatives in the present for the future. Without the exercise of the creative imagination, there can be no hope. It is not enough to protest. Instead, protest must be accompanied by alternatives, well-worked-out policies and realistic plans through the exercise of imagination.

Imagination in this context of hope is the enemy of absolutes, especially the absolutes of history, politics and religion that paralyse us in the present. There is nothing preordained about the injustices and inequalities of the present. Instead, imagination has the capacity to offer alternatives to the political status quo. Further, it is imagination that provides the springboard for action in the present. In addition, imagination can be the healer of the hopeless, especially those who suffer from mental illness. It is not too much imagination, but too little imagination, says Lynch (1965), that causes stress, anxiety and desolation.

It took the genius of Patrick Kavanagh (1992) to teach us that

> On the stem of memories,
>
> Imaginations flourish.

It is, therefore, on the back of contrast experiences, the role of the empathetic memory in reopening history and the power of the creative imagination to see alternative horizons that it becomes possible for secularists and believers to form a coalition of hope.

The Inclusive Shape of Christian Hope

It would be theologically wrong to suggest that Christian hope stands in opposition to human hope. These two hopes are closely connected, and yet different. Two examples may help to illustrate this point. The *Pastoral Constitution on the Church in the Modern World* from the Second Vatican Council (1965a) contains the seeds of a theology of hope at different levels. First of all, it points out in the opening paragraph that

> The joys and hopes, the grief and anguish of the
> people of our time, especially those who are poor
> or afflicted, are the joys and hopes, the grief and
> anguish of the followers of Christ as well. Nothing
> that is genuinely human fails to find an echo in their
> hearts.

The punchline in this statement is that nothing which is genuinely human fails to find an echo in the heart of Christian hope. Christian hope and human hope can unite around what is 'genuinely human' in addressing the grief and anguish of humanity.

Secondly, the same document (1965b) points out explicitly that Christian hope is not exempt from responsibility for developing the well-being of this life. 'It is a mistake', the Council states, indeed it is 'one of the gravest errors of our time' for those who believe in another world to neglect their responsibilities for this world. Here, the Council was reacting against the Marxist critique of religion as the opium of the people. In the contrast, the Council sought to make it clear that Christian hope embraces earthly responsibilities and should unite with all who are committed to these responsibilities.

What is distinctive and different about Christian hope is that it takes its inspiration and direction from the person of the crucified and risen Christ. Christian hope is Christocentric in structure. There are different dimensions to this Christocentric character of Christian hope.

There is, first of all, a historical dimension to Christian hope. Christian hope seeks to keep alive the memory of Jesus Christ at a number of levels, as noted by other contributors. There is the memory of Jesus the prophet and social reformer, the one who began his mission proclaiming good news to the poor, release to captives, sight to the blind and freedom to the oppressed (*Lk 4:16ff*). This mission and ministry of Jesus is summed up in parables under the imaginative vision of the coming reign of God, a reign of God already dawning in the life of Jesus in the present and promised in the future. During his life, Jesus put this vision into practice through a number of subversive actions: healing the hopeless, the reconciliation of outsiders, mercy and forgiveness for outcasts, an inclusive table fellowship, a cleansing of the temple, a washing of the feet and a new Passover meal. This imaginative vision and praxis of Jesus was directed at both society and religion. No one is exempt from the prophetic critique of this social and religious reformer. Christian hope, therefore, seeks to keep alive this memory of Jesus Christ, what some call the 'dangerous memory' of Jesus and others the 'liberating memory' of Jesus. There is much in the historical life of Jesus Christ that is of interest and relevance to human hope: attention to the plight of the poor, feeding the hungry, a commitment to justice, the promotion of freedom, the reform of society and religion.

A second layer to the Christ-centred character of Christian hope is the way it is played out in the historical drama of the life, death and Resurrection of Jesus. This unity of death and Resurrection holds together a number of tensions surrounding the shape, colour and rhythm of Christian hope. The shape of Christian hope is cruciform. The cross is at the centre of Christian hope. There is no way around the suffering and death that were a part of the life of Jesus and are a part of the human condition. The colour of

Christian hope is a 'bright-darkness'. Christian hope embraces the darkness of life and death in search for the light of Resurrection. The rhythm of Christian hope is the paschal process of dying and rising, of passing over from one place and returning to another, of decentring the self to recentre the self on the crucified and risen Christ.

A third layer to the Christocentric character of Christian hope is the claim that the Resurrection of Christ is the ground of Christian hope, and it is here that secularists and believers will differ most. The bodily Resurrection of Christ from the dead represents symbolically the goal of human life and the destiny of creation: the risen Christ in the New Testament is described as 'the first-born of all creation' (*Col 1:15*), 'the first-born from the dead' (*Col 1:18*; see also *Rom 8:29* and *Acts 26:23*), and 'the first-fruits of those who have died' (*1 Cor 15:20, 23*).

The Resurrection of Christ from the dead gives a glimpse of the goal of the spiritual energy that drove the unfolding of the cosmos, the evolution of biological life, and the historical drama of human existence, appearing now in a new mode of unimaginable creativity, splendour and beauty. As such, the Resurrection is the transformation of the unity of spirit and matter, of nature and grace, and of the love and sacrifice that animated the life of Jesus.

Moreover, the Resurrection implies that humanity, history and creation have a future, promising us

+ that the unfolding of the universe and the evolution of humanity are not ultimately rudderless, random events;

+ that the human within this unfolding is not just a spark in the evolutionary spiral that one day will burn out;

✝ that the beauty of planet earth is not simply a shooting star destined to disappear into the empty space of dark matter.

The fourth and final layer of the Christocentric content of Christian hope is the claim by the Second Vatican Council (1965c) that Christ is the exemplar of what it means to be human. 'In Christ light is shed on the mystery of humankind ... Christ discloses humankind to itself and manifests its sublime calling'. Christ lived life to the full – a life of self-giving service to his fellow human beings and the divine Other – and in doing this he showed us what it means to be fully human. At the centre of his life, there was the magnetism of love, not a sentimental love but the self-sacrificial love that led to Calvary and culminated in the Resurrection. If we believe in the fruitfulness of love, then we are already on the way to belief in the Resurrection.

There is enough common ground between human hopes and Christian hope to initiate a new national conversation, and at the same time there are differences which are more complementary than contradictory.

GLOBAL ECONOMIC INSECURITY AND IRELAND'S VULNERABILITY

DAVID BEGG

Introduction

In the film *The Wizard of Oz* Dorothy, having been swept up in a tornado, says to her little dog, 'Toto, I've a feeling we're not in Kansas anymore'. This may resonate with many people as they ponder the state of the world today. The year 2016 is likely to be remembered, if not as a critical juncture in the course of economic history, then, at the very least, as an inflection point. One commentator, writing in the aftermath of the US Presidential Election, described it as 'the bonfire of the certainties'.

Something quite profound is happening in the advanced democracies of our world. The forces at work are cultural, political, economic and social, driven in part by technological change. Artificial intelligence seems to be on the cusp of a breakthrough, something which may bring great benefits, but which is also potentially hugely disruptive, particularly of labour markets. Whereas the replacement of labour by technology is something which has been going on for two hundred years, the arrival of artificial intelligence suggests that the process is approaching its apogee. In the twentieth century, automation was highly destructive of manufacturing employment and the working class; in this century artificial intelligence is about to inflict similar damage on the middle class. Two words have recently become fashionable in political and economic discourse: 'disruption' and 'resilience'. The former stands for radical economic and social innovation, while the latter stands for adaptive adjustment, which may be more or less voluntary. These words are euphemisms which may conceal the potential for a high degree of social upheaval.

The present era is characterised by a number of secular trends – declining growth, growing inequality and rising debt – which appear to be mutually reinforcing. Low growth contributes to inequality by intensifying distributional conflict; inequality dampens growth by restricting effective demand; high levels of debt increase the possibility of another financial crisis, and so on. On the other hand, if low growth rates continue, the outcome, if properly managed, could help to avoid ecological disaster. But this would require robust institutions to manage new cleavages and distributional conflicts in society.

This is the context for an evaluation, in this chapter, of the possibilities for imagining a more sustainable and socially just development model for our country. Ireland, however, is a very small open economy and its fortunes are contingent on stability in Europe and the wider world. Accordingly, it is first proposed to look at the bigger picture.

Global Economic Stability

'The Great Moderation' was a phrase coined in 2004 by the former chairman of the US Federal Reserve, Ben Bernanke, to describe the absence of volatility in the business cycle between the mid-1980s and 2008. It turned out to be a chimera. Politicians believed that stability had been achieved by policy alone, but that notion was blown away by the collapse of Lehman Brothers Bank on 15 September 2008. It is now clear that the stability over the previous twenty years was sustained by a combination of an altered power balance between capital and labour, the deflationary impact of China, and the rise of cheap credit. When the Soviet Union collapsed and China became capitalist by decree, an extra 1.5 billion people were added to the existing global workforce of 960 million. Almost overnight, the global relationship between capital and labour was massively tilted in favour of capital, strategically weakening the bargaining power of workers in every country (Mason 2009).

The advanced economies have been affected by slow growth, de-industrialisation, high unemployment, falling labour-force participation and rising inequality. To a large extent, this burden has fallen on relatively unskilled people and has fuelled anger about mass immigration. While the threat to unskilled employment caused by technology is difficult to halt, bad mistakes were made in not trying to ensure that the gains from economic growth were more widely shared. The financial developments in 2008 and the subsequent Eurozone crisis were, however, the decisive events.

In reality, the era of market liberalisation turned out to be also the era of financial crisis, culminating in the biggest and most important of them in 2008 (Wolf 2014a). A crucial aspect of the crisis was the rise of global imbalances, with emerging economies deciding to export capital to advanced countries that the latter proved unable to use effectively. The abundance of liquidity and low interest rates encouraged financial institutions and asset holders to try to increase the rate of return on their portfolios by increased leverage at the cost of higher risks. In summary, the global financial crisis emanated from the conjunction of widespread financial fragility and a lopsided globalisation process, proceeding amidst large financial imbalances. A compounding factor was the inadequacy of regulation and supervision, together with the mismanagement of large financial institutions (Gylfason et al. 2010).

The response to the crisis undermined belief in the system's fairness. The banks were bailed out, but ordinary people lost their jobs and homes. In the process, the unstated compact on which democracy rests – that elites can earn huge incomes or enjoy influence and power as long as they demonstrate competence in providing for the weak of society – unravelled.

The resulting political vacuum was filled by new political actors from the far left and the radical right. On the left, the first manifestation of this was the annihilation of the Greek Socialist Party, Pasok, and its replacement by the more left-wing Syriza. The same phenomenon occurred in Spain, with the emergence of Podemos, and, in Britain, Jeremy Corbyn, despite having only minority support in the parliamentary party, won the leadership of the Labour Party and comprehensively defeated a subsequent challenge to his leadership.

Without doubt, the most significant achievement of radical right populism was the election of President Donald Trump and his post-election repudiation of political norms of behaviour, epitomised by the withdrawal of the US from the Paris Climate Change Agreement. It all seems a long way from the hubristic predictions of the dominance of liberal democracy, as outlined by Francis Fukuyama (1992) in his book, *The End of History*, published in the wake of the collapse of the Soviet Union. Neoclassical economic orthodoxy holds that depressions are the result of an exogenous shock, rather than forces generated within the system. This is an orthodoxy epitomised by the 'Washington Consensus', but cast into disrepute by the 2008 crisis. As a result, the ideas of Hyman Minsky (1986) are now receiving renewed attention. Minsky showed that speculative bubbles, and the financial collapses that followed them, are an integral part of modern capitalism. That is, they are not the result of accidents or poor decision-making, but a fundamental and recurring feature of economic life once the financial system is deregulated.

Martin Wolf (2014b) makes the point that the solutions of three decades ago have morphed into the problems of today. Acknowledging that this is not a new experience in human history, he suggests, all the same, that it is particularly likely to happen when a philosophy is taken to extremes. In his words:

> Liberal democracy is, I believe, now threatened by financial instability and rising inequality as it was by the high inflation and squeezed profits of the 1970s. In learning lessons from that era, we have, perhaps inevitably, made mistakes in this one.

The financial systems of the high-income economies shifted from stability to extreme fragility over the decades before the crisis. This is not really disputed. The question is, why? An extraordinary feature of global financial instability is the extent to which the system was underpinned by ideas about how the world's most so-phisticated economies and financial systems should work – ideas that turned out to be nonsense. It is worth looking a bit deeper into the power of ideas, which we will do in the next section.

The Influence of Ideas

John Maynard Keynes (1936) once famously wrote that 'it is ideas, not vested interests, which are dangerous for good or evil'. He was right. Economists and policy makers need to rethink their understanding of the world in important respects. The pre-crisis conventional wisdom, manifested in notions of the 'Great Moderation', stands revealed as complacent, even vainglorious.

In their book, *The Fall of the Celtic Tiger* (2013), Donal Dono-van and Antoin Murphy comprehensively describe the influence of ideas, such as the new classical macroeconomics (NCM) and efficient market hypothesis (EMH). The former is a develop-ment of the monetarist thinking of Milton Friedman. At its core, it argues, contrary to the Keynesian view, that macroeconomic policy is impotent. From the 1970s, this became the dominant paradigm taught in universities. As graduates found their way into key institutions, including the European Central Bank (ECB), the influence of NCM ideas became quite profound. Its rejection of any kind of economic stimulus implied that independent Central Banks should be used to take monetary and fiscal policy out of the hands of the politicians.

The EMH became the soulmate of NCM. It is the brainchild of another Chicago economist, Eugene Fama, and it holds that as-set prices will reflect all the relevant information that is available, so that market actors cannot make excessive gains from trading.

Markets, by this reasoning, are self- correcting and adjust for any change in information. The logical implication is that only light-touch regulation is necessary. The insouciance encouraged by rational expectations and efficient market hypotheses made regulators and investors careless.

Wolfgang Streeck (2014) asserts that there is a core idea, based on a utopian ideal, which seeks to depoliticise the economy and insulate it from any form of democratic participation. In this view, the expectation is that, in time, people would come to regard the distributional outcomes of free markets as fair, or at least without alternative.

It is not unreasonable to speculate that the political upheaval we are now experiencing is a reaction, at least in part, to the consequences of these ideas. It is interesting to note that much of what constitutes modern macroeconomic governance today was established relatively recently. Direct inflation targeting is common today, but was unknown before the 1990s. Also, until the 1990s, Central Bank independence was the exception (Munchau 2016).

Whither Europe?

The institutional architecture of Economic and Monetary Union (EMU) is consistent with the NCM/EMF philosophy. Under the Maastricht Treaty, the ECB became a powerful independent institution, with the single objective of price stability, leaving growth and employment to be determined by market forces.

The clear lesson of the 2008 crisis is that the institutional architecture of EMU is deficient. A currency union is not sustainable on its own without a banking, fiscal and, ultimately, political union. For most of its history, European integration had the support of a permissive consensus from the people of Europe. That consensus was eviscerated in the wake of the financial crisis of 2008.

In truth, Europe is confronted by existential crises on many fronts. Anti-European sentiment is undermining the established political order in many countries. Europe faces threats from terrorism and immigration, both of which are proving difficult to manage. Its broader security has been compromised by Russian efforts to change the borders of Europe. Having a mercantilist nuclear power to deal with, in circumstances of doubts about continuing US support for NATO, is a challenge for a political entity that never managed a coherent foreign policy. A deal between Trump and Putin to accept Moscow's revanchism would, in effect, overturn the security settlement that has prevailed since 1945. Where, one wonders, would this leave Poland, a nation that under its current authoritarian leadership expects western partners to underwrite its security, even as it repudiates their democratic values?

Economic growth in the EU is increasing only slowly, despite the ECB buying government and corporate bonds to the amount of €80bn a month for some time now. This level of quantitative easing is hardly sustainable in the long run, but neither is there a willingness to allow fiscal policy to take on the task of stimulating the economy.

The political situation in Europe has stabilised somewhat, with the expected gains by right-wing populist parties in Austria, the Netherlands and France not materialising. Nevertheless, the postwar party system has been shaken. The success of the Liberal Party in the Netherlands was achieved by tacking to the right on immigration. In Britain, the Conservative Party has eclipsed UKIP largely by adopting a hard Brexit stance. Although Macron came out on top in France, it is worth remembering that he secured only 24% of the vote in the first round, just three percentage points ahead of Le Pen. He won the second round by a landslide, not because he swept French voters off their feet, but because many could not bring themselves to vote for the National Front. It will not be easy for Macron. Like Britain and the US, France remains deeply divided between those who favour a liberal, open society and those who seek closed politics and borders, between supporters of European integration and proponents of nationalism and protectionism. Like Macron, Matteo Renzi was thirty-nine when he became Italy's Prime Minister in 2014 on a promise of change. But he did not succeed and soon became unpopular. In Italy, the Social Democratic PD Party remains the only pro-European party, and anti-Euro populists are well placed to win the next election.

Imbalances within Europe remain a problem. Germany's surplus is €754bn, while Italy's deficit is €359bn. This does not look sustainable. One day, Italy may be led by a party in favour of withdrawal from the Euro. If and when that happens, Euro exit could turn into a self-fulfilling prophesy. There could be a run on Italy's banks and government bonds.

Of course, none of this may happen, but there is uncertainty in the air. For instance, as European heads of government gathered in Rome at the end of March 2017 to mark the sixtieth anniversary of the signing of the Treaty of Rome, it was remarkable how the celebrations were somewhat muted. Pope Francis met with the leaders and exhorted them to remain united for the journey and to continue with 'renewed enthusiasm and confidence'. He impressed upon them that 'Europe finds new hope in solidarity, which is also the most effective antidote to populism'.

The problem is that, in trying to get to grips with these challenges, Europe is in a kind of decision trap. The further European integration progresses, particularly as led by EMU, the more it infringes on the basic rights, provisions and redistributive functions of member states. Moreover, because of the great variations in welfare models across the enlarged EU, and because welfare is largely a domestic competence, there is no effective institutional balance to the power and independence of the ECB. Given the practical difficulties of creating any kind of institutional balance to the ECB, the only alternative – and it would be a difficult one for Germany to swallow – would be to change the remit of the ECB to bring it more into line with that of the Federal Reserve Board in the United States.

That may sound strange, because Europe is generally regarded as embracing higher levels of social solidarity than the US. But the fact is that, under the Humphrey Hawkins Act of 1978, the FED is required to take on board the Government's economic and social goals, something not required by the ECB's sole concern with price stability. Notwithstanding that the ECB has, in practice, pushed the boundaries of its mandate to try to stimulate the European economy, the institutional imbalance between monetary and social objectives is so egregious that it is hard to envisage any popular revival of public support for deeper integration until the concept of social Europe is seen to have a higher priority. It would be a mistake if complacency over recent election outcomes should cause policy makers to conclude that the danger to the European integration project has passed.

Ireland, Britain and Europe

Ireland's future is highly contingent on what happens in Europe. In economic terms, the reason is that the foreign industrial sector increased significantly after 1986, when the passage of the Single European Act made it very attractive for American multinationals to use Ireland as a base to access the single market. On the other hand, the UK remains an important market for indigenous industry. In fact, Ireland is Britain's fifth largest trading partner. In 2012, 43% of exports from Irish companies went to the UK, while the corresponding figure for Foreign Direct Investment (FDI) companies was 12%. Supply chain linkages are also important for Ireland, as UK wholesalers often supply the Irish market, and UK supermarkets have a high market share in Ireland. Gas and electricity markets between the two countries are also coupled. At this stage, there have been many reports analysing the potential economic impact of Brexit on Ireland, but it would appear to represent a permanent loss to GDP of up to 3% (see, for example, Booth et al. 2015).

In many respects, Ireland is an outlier in Europe. It is the sole liberal market economy within the Eurozone, the most distant geographically of the northern member states from the heart of Europe, and one of only three countries not part of the continental land mass. The Irish economy cycles are out of phase with those of the core continental states of the Eurozone because of Ireland's heavy export and investment dependence on Britain and the United States. It has low levels of intra-industry Euro-area trade. This misalignment means that Ireland's interest rate requirements are different from those of other countries, and unlikely ever to be a priority for ECB monetary policy. Despite this unique risk exposure, EMU membership never became a highly politicised issue amongst the mainstream political parties. It was always assumed that Britain would join the single currency at some stage. It didn't, and now intends to leave the EU altogether. The bottom line here is that the policy assumptions underpinning our relations with Europe were always flawed.

There is a danger that the current strong performance of the Irish economy could disguise certain underlying vulnerabilities. The Economic and Social Research Institute (ESRI) estimates that the economy grew by 4.8% in 2016 and will expand by 3.8% in 2017 and 3.6% in 2018. It is also predicting robust consumption and investment growth in 2017 and a fall in unemployment to 6.4% by the end of the year (McQuinn et al. 2017). It is also clear that many social deficits remain, however, following the 2008 crisis. This is most evident in the areas of healthcare, housing and infrastructure. An ageing demographic has clear implications for healthcare and pensions, in circumstances where only 47% of the working population have any kind of occupational or private pension beyond the State Welfare pension. When added to the high level of public and private debt, the uncertainty of Brexit, the potential risk to FDI from policy changes in the US, and a more active anti-avoidance corporate tax drive from the EU and OECD, a disconcerting picture emerges. Professor John Fitzgerald (2017) argues that there is a tendency to exaggerate the importance of foreign multinationals in the Irish economic model and to underestimate the strength and importance of Irish firms in driving growth in the economy. He believes that Ireland has gone a long way to wean itself off dependence on the low corporate tax regime attracting multinationals, and that Irish success is now more broadly based. Nevertheless, we are in a place where the twin pillars of an industrial policy which has been in place for sixty years – FDI and UK market access for agricultural products principally – can no longer be relied on with certainty. Taken in conjunction with the social challenges already mentioned, and a tendency towards boom and bust economic cycles, Ireland's development model lacks the characteristics of sustainability.

Since independence, Ireland has made great progress in many ways, but it is a sobering reality that the country faced economic desolation on four occasions: in the 1930s, 1950s, 1980s and more recently following 2008. In hindsight, the most sustainable period was between 1994 and 2001, when growth was based on a competitive economy supporting a strong exporting manufacturing base. Genuinely developmentalist policies were assisted by the stabilising influence of social partnership, together with the stimulus from EU structural and cohesion funds and increased FDI consequent upon the 1986 Single European Act. Currency devaluations in 1986 and 1993 were also significant, as was increased female participation in the labour force. Developmentalism is defined by Eva Paus (2012) as the use of active industrial policies to advance social capabilities. She laments that the policy coherence underpinning this approach did not survive into the 2000s.

Recapturing the developmentalism of the 1990s and redefining our relationship with Britain and Europe is the key to achieving sustainability. If we are willing to admit it, the truth is that, with a few exceptions, the big vision of Europe did not excite. We were motivated by a desire to maximise the economic benefits of membership and to assert our independence from Britain. Britain was regarded as our closest ally in Europe, with both countries often working together to block Commission initiatives. This joint action, it must be said, was usually in the area of social policy, viewed as undermining our respective liberal market economy models. That kind of relationship with Britain is no longer possible, and with that reality, we have reached the denouement of the independence debate in an unexpected way.

Instead, we have to begin now to engage with the European integration project in a wholly different way. We have to take it seriously. We also have to re-orientate the indigenous pillar of our economy to reduce dependence on UK markets. Enterprise Ireland has always operated in the shadow of the IDA. It needs a narrative of its own mission which reflects this new reality.

Where might we look for inspiration in confronting this challenge? The Nordic countries' experience might make a rewarding study. In the 1950s two economists, Rudolf Meidner and Gosta Rehn, designed a model for a highly productive economy which was, more or less, adopted by most countries in that region. Today, they are among the most economically efficient, competitive and socially cohesive countries in the world. Yet, like Ireland, they are small open economies exposed to the ravages of international markets. They are characterised by a capacity to respond quickly to changing economic conditions, while maintaining high levels of social protection. When, for example, the Soviet Union collapsed, Finland had to completely re-orientate its economy towards the European Centre. It succeeded very well. Ireland does not face a challenge on quite this scale, but a formidable one all the same. The great attraction of the Nordic model is that it offers the possibility of having a market economy without having to have a market society.

Conclusion

Public policy in Ireland remains pro-Europe. Even though it has been strained by the Commission's attitude to Ireland's corporate tax policy, this is unlikely to change, Brexit notwithstanding. What might cause a rethink would be an Italian opt-out from the Euro.

For all its faults, the EU is the only political entity concerned with the collective issues of welfare sustainability as a public good. It is also the embodiment of unique Christian values, exemplified by two outstanding public figures, Pope Francis and Chancellor Angela Merkel, the latter coming from the Protestant tradition. It is worth recalling Ms Merkel's words in response to the election of Donald Trump:

> Germany and the US are tied by their values: democracy, freedom, respect for the rule of law and the dignity of humankind – independent of origin, skin colour, gender, sexual orientation or political views.

The contrast is striking. Ms Merkel is comfortable talking about the values that sustain our civilisation; Mr Trump does deals.

Pope Francis and Angela Merkel, almost alone in Europe today, inspire Christians to try to live up to what the German theologian, Johann Baptist Metz (1992) called 'The dangerous memory of Jesus Christ'. It is a dangerous memory because it demands of us to be 'doers of the word'.

This is a theology rooted in praxis. It surely implies active engagement in public affairs in pursuit of the common good. Recent years have seen a coarseness enter public discourse exacerbated by social media. The only effective way to counter the demagoguery, populism and anti-politics of this era is for citizens to participate more actively in society, to reboot an active form of civic republicanism.

The Europe of today falls a long way short of the ideal, but it worth fighting to reform it to try to achieve its possibilities. That might mean Ireland taking its involvement in Europe seriously, perhaps for the first time. What in practical terms should we try to achieve? The Catholic writer, Paul Vallely (1998), put it well when he opined that the great challenge of our times is to combine economic efficiency, social justice and individual liberty in a new balance, a balance which we in the modern age have lost.

There is now an extensive literature on the varieties of capitalism to be found in the world today. This school can be traced back to Karl Polanyi's canonical work of political economy, published in 1944, entitled *The Great Transformation*. It is of particular relevance to this question of balance in the context of globalisation. Globalisation has caused a deep erosion of social regimes which in the past, at least to some degree, limited the commodification of what Polanyi described as the three fictitious commodities of labour, land and money. Polanyi's thesis is that it is in the logic of capitalist development and its utopia of a self-regulating market that, in order to continue its advance, it must strive ultimately to commodify everything. Labour, land and money, however, if they are to retain their practical value, can be commodified only within narrow limits. Complete commodification destroys them and thereby obstructs, rather than enhances, capital accumulation. The evidence can be seen in the trend towards precarious work, accelerating consumption and destruction of the natural environment.

Everything that needs to be said about the environment is

said in the papal encyclical, *Laudato Si'*. With respect to money, the evidence of commodification lies in the transformation of debt into a tradeable commodity, with ultimate consequences for homelessness, which has become an existential social problem. Keeping labour, land and money from complete commodification, and thereby protecting them from abuse, requires the authority of government, but that has, to a large extent, been undermined by globalisation. The small open economies of northern Europe have come closest to the variety of capitalism capable of achieving the best balance in order to mitigate these pressures of globalisation. The full implications of making a transition to a new development model on Nordic lines are beyond the scope of this chapter, but interested readers will find the concept explored comprehensively in a separate publication (Begg 2016).

BEYOND THE SLOGANS: FUTURE PROSPECTS, PRESENT DILEMMAS

MICHAEL CRONIN

Man is a believing animal and to few, if any, is it given to criticise the foundations of belief 'intelligently' ... To inquire into the ultimates behind accepted group values is obscene and sacrilegious: objective inquiry is an attempt to uncover the nakedness of man, his soul as well as his body, his deeds, his cultures, and his very gods. Certainly the large general [economics] courses should be prevented from raising any question about objectivity, but should assume the objectivity of the slogans they inculcate, as a sacred feature of the system.

The author of these words was Frank Knight, a founder of the market-oriented Chicago school of economics, writing in 1932. In his view, economics was not to be just an article of faith, it was to be faith itself. Critical questions around the 'foundations of belief' were to be shunned as courting heresy, and first-year students, like the general public, were to be inculcated with slogans as 'gospel truths'. This sacralisation of the market has continued to this day, as Harvey Cox points out (2016), with the notion of the divine control of human destiny giving way, in the secular age, to the belief that markets ought to and do control our fates.

Where there is no alternative, there is, in essence, no real democracy. Democratic choice in this scenario is reduced to a choice among competing versions of the market control of societies, rather than the social control of markets. The difficulty for market absolutists is that the slogans are proving fatal both to social cohesion and ecological sustainability. Consider the present situation, for example, where eight individuals hold the same wealth as the combined wealth of the planet's poorest 3.6 billion people (Oxfam International 2017), or the fact that CO_2 emissions in 2015 averaged 60% higher than at the time of the first Intergovernmental Panel on Climate Change report in 1990 (Anderson 2015).

The reduction of all social relations to market logic – what Richard Norgaard has called 'economism' – demands, in effect, a new kind of apostasy, a refusal from the point of view of environmental sustainability and social justice to allow the foundations and consequences of current economic beliefs to go unchallenged. Without functioning life-support systems, the planet will cease to be and the economy with it. There is no point in free trade in a landscape of desolation, where extinction forecloses any possibility of freedom. No markets flourish on a dead planet. So how might we think about challenging the false idols of economism? In this present age, what theses might we need to hammer on the cathedral doors of high finance?

Individuals

Fundamental to the orthodoxy of economism is a belief in the freely choosing, fully informed, rational individual. From an ecological standpoint, however, the autonomous individual is more of a fetish than a fact. All individuals are connected to the rest of the world, not only through their genetic relationships to other species and their carbon composition dating back to the Big Bang, but all individuals owe their existence and survival to the air, water and food resources that are made available by the planet. Not only this, no serious social scientist can take the notion of the atomistic individual seriously, as humans are, from the moment of conception, profoundly dependent on the care and solicitude of others. Individuals make choices, but they do so in social contexts, with impacts on themselves and on others, and on the non-human environments with which they are inextricably bound up. As Richard Norgaard (2015) points out:

> With increasing maturity, we come to realise that who we have become and what our desires are depend on the choices we have made and the people we have known. Our own essence and those of the people closest to us are dependent on and affected by these choices. Economists ignore this reality and worship the 'freedom to choose', treating obligations to wider society as costs to be avoided.

The narcissism that results from the flattered human subject of individualism also extends to a disregard for the non-human. The universe is filled with objects to be consumed rather than subjects to be communed with, so that earth, wind, water and fire – in the form of soil, air, water and fossil fuels – are used and abused with elemental profligacy. If we start, not with the unreal fiction of the isolated subject but with the environmental reality of the connected being, we realise that the task of economics means ensuring the viable allocation of resources for the survival of our planet's species, and indeed of the planet itself. According proper legal recognition to the non-human world becomes the task of jurisprudence, so that the fate of other species and of the non-human world is not subordinated to the narrow instrumental interests of humans.

The notion of the fully informed economic agent acting in terms of rational self-interest needs to be questioned, in view of the kinds of information that are normally brought to bear on the making of decisions. Simply comparing the price of goods and services, as if in a supermarket trolley, is totally inadequate in making informed decisions. If we are to become aware of the full, long-term ecological costs and consequences of choices made in the areas of housing, transport, food production and IT usage, we will need a much deeper notion of what consumer education might involve than that. In other words, the way in which we think of the human as economic agent has to change profoundly if there is to be any substantive move towards a carbon-neutral society. If we accept that the nature of economic agency needs to be rethought in the age of human-induced climate change, what might be the wider structures in which these subjects would flourish in a sustainable manner?

Enterprise

One wider structure that needs to change, because it determines so much else that may or may not change, is business itself. The conventional primacy given to the shareholder perspective, where the only metric used to evaluate success is financial return on investment, is coming under intense scrutiny, not only from civil society activists, but also from within business circles. As three leading experts in the field of business management and finance pointed out in a recent work:

> The myopic focus of the business world on maximizing shareholder wealth is now fair game for critics, given its short-termism and lack of sustainability, its neglect of social or environmental impacts, its fostering of economic inequality, and its tendency to incentivise unethical and unprincipled behaviour (Sternad et al. 2016a).

If a primary goal of business is to create value, then it is the nature of that value which needs to be re-examined. Businesses need to make a profit. If they do not, they simply disappear. There is an increasing realisation, however, that it is possible to be both profitable and purpose-driven. In the words of Sternad, Kennelly and Bradley, there are more and more entrepreneurs and business leaders for whom, 'making meaning is at least as important as making money'. That is to say, purpose-driven enterprises – and these include everything from Faber Castell, the German manufacturers of writing instruments, to the Italian coffee merchants illycaffè – are concerned that their businesses contribute to the overall social and ecological well-being of the societies and planet in which they live. To this end, the emphasis is less on immediate returns on short-term transactions and more on building long-term sustainable relationships. The notion of value is given a broader meaning to include, not just financial viability, but social responsibility, ecological stewardship and a commitment to equity. Michael Porter and Mark Kramer, writing in the *Harvard Business Review* (2011), argued for a notion of 'shared value', by which they meant the need for companies to focus on creating, not only monetary value, but societal value, by addressing the real needs of people and communities. The advantages are: more meaningful and equitable workplaces for employees, longer-term sustainable business models, more valuable products and services for consumers, and more ethically rewarding forms of investment for shareholders. Moving from purpose to prosperity or from the bottom line to betterment entails a reincorporation of businesses and enterprises into a broader ecological project of social or environmental benefit. This need not take the form of 'greenwashing' or a slick organic rebranding exercise. Rather, it can look to the example of many successful businesses throughout the world that have embraced the notion of shared or real value. Central to this expanded notion of value is: long-term orientation, the formation of durable relationships, the recognition of limits, investment in local place, the cultivation of learning communities and the development of responsible leadership to achieve these aims (Sternad et al. 2016b). A wider and more imaginative conception of the enterprise landscape also means that a sense of ethical investment and collective ownership, together with a much greater sensitivity to the social and environmental consequences of the economic activity, needs to feature more generally in education. Cynicism about market hegemony or despair about corporate control in the present should not foreclose possibilities for the future.

Demand

Paul D. Raskin (2006) tries to imagine a world that has taken seriously the dire predicament facing our species, with the ever-growing threat of climate change. The imagined place of writing is 'Mandela City' and the year is 2084. A new set of values underpins the entire edifice of society: 'Consumerism, individualism, and domination of nature – the dominant values of yesteryear – have given way to a new triad: quality of life, human solidarity, and ecological sensibility'. Issues of governance and new forms of geopolitical organisation loom large in his utopian blueprint. Organisation on the basis of nations has given way to the primacy of regions, and these regions tend to cluster around three types, 'Agoria', 'Ecodemia' and 'Arcadia'. Agoria represents a type of advanced social democracy. Ecodemia is akin to a radical socialism, with an emphasis on collective ownership and participation. Arcadia is the expression of an essentially libertarian outlook, with the emphasis on self-reliant communities, face-to-face democracy and community engagement. Raskin is mindful also of the pressing questions of wealth creation and income redistribution. He imagines the answers to these questions as taking two forms: changing the organisation of enterprise and changing the nature of demand. The changing nature of enterprise, of course, can in part be a response to the changing nature of demand. In terms of a demand-side ecology, Raskin tries to express the emergence of a new demand culture, leading to a shrinking human ecological footprint. 'Changing consumption patterns have decreased the share of tangible goods in the world economy, in favour of dematerialised sectors such as services, arts, knowledge, and crafts production.' What Raskin is advocating is a shift from a society largely preoccupied with wealth, in the form of the acquisition of material goods, to one that is primarily focused on the notion of fulfilment through the enjoyment of intangibles.

Of course, enthusiasm for the 'dematerialised' needs to be tempered by ecological realism as to the material consequences of the 'virtual'. Information technology consumes vast quantities of energy and is a voracious user of precious metals and non-renewable resources (Cronin 2017). Caution is also needed in privileging intangible fulfilment over material wealth on a planet of gross inequality and shocking disparities in income. It is worth bearing in mind, however, that ecological sustainability is bound up with social justice. The forces that fuel environmental destruction are also those driving income inequality. As John Bellamy Foster (2015) notes, 'a shift away from capital accumulation and towards a system of meeting collective needs based on the principle of enough is obviously impossible in any meaningful sense under the regime of capital accumulation'.

A major difficulty with any ecological transition is the taboo on limitation. As Thomas Berry observes (1999), 'Some ancient force in the Western psyche seems to perceive limitation as an obstacle to be eliminated, rather than as a strengthening discipline'. Any move forward is always presented as dismantling barriers, removing obstacles, challenging limits. Everything from sportswear to economic development is branded as an exercise in removing limitations. Our post-Enlightenment sensibility finds the idea of being limited in any way as intolerable – an affront to our freedom to choose and now, more importantly, to consume. However, the conclusions of the COP21 Agreement, signed in Paris in December 2015, are clear. The prime objective is to contain the

increase in global temperature to below 2°C relative to pre-indus-
trial levels, but calls are made for energetic measures to contain
the rise to 1.5°C. The 'global emissions ceiling' must be reached
'in the shortest possible time', with countries targeting emissions
neutrality in the second half of the twenty-first century (ENGIE
2016). The European Union's stated aim to cut greenhouse gases
by 40% by 2030 – an aim regularly contested by Ireland – shows
that the efforts required in terms of reducing the use of energy,
and hence consumption, are enormous.

This crisis has resulted, of course, from our historic refusal to
recognise the fact that the planet itself is setting limits to its ability to absorb the unbridled use of fossil fuels and the relentless
assault on biodiversity. In other words, notions of 'progress' and
'growth' cannot any longer be equated with the endless production and consumption of material goods that ignore the natural
limits to planetary sustainability. Bringing about such a profound
change in our psyche and sensibility demands nothing less than
an ethical revolution in our way of doing business, running our
economy and defining the nature of private and public goods.
To this end, it is crucial that all groups in society who share a
common and urgent concern for the well-being of the planet are
mobilised. The challenge to our sense of reality and to our values
needs to take place at such a profound level that it is the origin
and meaning of existence itself that is in play. In this respect,
there is a need to reconsider radically the anthropological foundations of the current economic order. We need to think differently
about what it is to be human, in particular, and about our impact
on the entire geo-biological order of the planet, and how this
needs to change to ensure our survival as a species.

Knowledge

In the age of the 'knowledge economy' and the 'smart society', the asceticism of demand-side ecology can seem disturbingly retrograde. The project can smack of neo-Luddism, a nostalgic hankering after an obscurantist past. More worryingly, scepticism about the promise of the growth economy could suggest a hostility or antipathy to research, innovation and, indeed, knowledge itself (Phillips 2015). This is manifestly not the case, if only because the 'production and reproduction of our species-being, whatever it may be, has to be a central concern of any critical knowledge' (McKenzie Wark 201a). The challenge of the Anthropocene – the human-induced era of climate change – is precisely the need to question deeply-held assumptions, to think the unthinkable and to develop new forms of knowledge that are responsive, not just to our current predicament, but to the planet that will be inherited by those who come after us. The need to orient knowledge to different ends by taking means seriously, requires, among other things, that we reconsider the infrastructures of knowledge. A key component of these infrastructures is provided by those institutions whose avowed aim is the support and promotion of research, namely universities. It might be asked, however, whether universities as they are currently constituted are capable of developing a critical knowledge that meets the current and future needs of the 'production and reproduction of our species-being'. In other words, is there not a sense in which taking seriously the ecological fallout of economism means challenging conventional assumptions about the current organisation of knowledge?

If one examines the evolution of the European university, it is possible to posit three stages of development. The first stage is the emergence of what might be termed the 'monarchical university'. The universities which emerged from the eleventh century onwards largely depended on royal patronage, not least in allowing for a degree of autonomy from Church authorities. The second stage in the development of these universities was the emergence of the 'national university', notably in the early nineteenth century, where the primary duty of the university was to prepare the future citizens of the nation-state (Readings 1997). The third stage was the emergence of the 'corporate university' in the latter half of the twentieth century, where the relative loss of economic sovereignty by individual nation-states, the rise of supra-national governance, the deregulation of markets and the global connectivity of Information and Communication Technology meant that universities conceived of themselves less as national public bodies and increasingly as transnational, corporate entities committed to maximizing the financial resources of the institution through competition in an international educational market (Collini 2012). The proliferation of rankings and other measures of comparison is an intrinsic part of the marketisation of education in a globalised world. If we are to avoid a dramatic depletion of the resources of the planet, it is necessary for us to develop alternative ways of thinking which challenge the core tenets of a shareholder-driven model of maximalist growth and financialised models of economic practice. Unfortunately, the financial crisis of 2008 did not fundamentally alter this model. Indeed, the rationale of austerity was employed to restore the orthodoxy of growth as a core value of economic and political activity (Lanchester 2010).

The reality is that the employment needs, the nutritional needs and the educational needs of the planet's inhabitants cannot be met by a growth model which is predicated on the unsustainable and destructive use of increasingly scarce resources, whether this be water, land, food or knowledge itself, corralled off in the auction rooms of the patents market. This is where we might speculate on the emergence of the 'transitional university', committed to a form of knowledge organisation directed to the creation of a carbon-neutral, sustainable and resilient economy and society. The transitional university is more ambitious in its conception than the 'green campus' model which, however laudable, confines itself to minimising the carbon footprint of individual institutions. The transitional university is one that responds to the radically changed circumstances of the Anthropocene, by developing forms of knowledge covering all domains of human activity – from medicine to jurisprudence, from philosophy to economics – as they interact with the human and non-human world. The transitional university is not a return to an idealised past of cloistered privilege but is, by definition, future-focused. As McKenzie Wark (2015b) says, 'There's no going back. There's only forward. It's a question of struggling to open another future besides this one which … has no future at all'. Organic farming, community-based agriculture, solar-hydrogen energy systems, urban planning, transport management, eco-jurisprudence: all of these suppose forms of expertise and a value base that have clear implications for the structures of knowledge that we embed in our institutions. Outlining the efforts needed to effect a successful transition to a sustainable economy and society, Richard Norgaard (2015) might equally be outlining the research agenda and ethical basis for the transitional university, when he speaks of supporting sustainable consumption and de-growth; promoting the commons paradigm;

working with religion to foster an ethic for an equitable and sustainable planet; furthering justice; improving the sciences; furthering agro-ecology; facilitating local markets; encouraging progressive forms of corporate ownership, governance and practice; and warning of limits and possibilities of tipping points.

Mobilising Hope

The impending ecological crisis points to the overwhelming need for Irish society to stand back, take stock and adopt the long view, if the many places that go to make up the planet – including Ireland – are to have a sustainable future. Standing back does not mean opting out but moving forward. Caring about what the past has to say and what the future has to bear means that what we do matters, and this should be ground for hope and not cause for despair. The opportunities for change in the current moment are immense. And they will have consequences. In seeking to go beyond the narrow, short-term practices of economism we need, in the words of Bruno Latour (2016), 'to re-establish ourselves on an Earth that has nothing to do with the protective borders of nation-states any more than an infinite horizon of globalisation'. Dealing with the inescapable urgency of climate change means that we must fundamentally rethink various aspects of our political, economic and social behaviour. Giving in to an apocalyptic vision of despair is a luxury neither we nor the planet can afford. We must look to all those sections of our society that are committed to a purposeful vision of the human, so that together we can mobilise that scarcest of all resources – hope – to create a future that will be there for all to enjoy.

A CHALLENGE TO THE CHURCHES

GERRY O'HANLON SJ

Introduction

In our joint position paper, 'The Signs of Our Times', we have outlined different dimensions of the crisis we are experiencing in Ireland and worldwide. We have indicated why we consider that the dominant narrative supporting the current status quo is spent, and why the making of an alternative narrative should have input from secular and religious voices, from poor and rich people, atheists and believers, scientists and philosophers, poets and theologians. What role might the Christian Churches have in this 'coalition of hope' as they contribute to a new project of human flourishing in Ireland? After all, are not the Churches themselves mired in crisis and often – in particular in the case of the Roman Catholic Church and its past dominant role in the formation of a flawed public morality – perceived as obstacles rather than aids to progress?

The dominant narrative of our times is undergirded by a kind of group bias masquerading as common sense. Bernard Lonergan (1970) speaks of the shortcomings of common sense at times of crisis: it is shot through with non-sense and it is incapable of adverting to the need for a new theoretical paradigm when the old one has broken down. We have argued that we are at such a juncture now. The neo-liberal economic model, with its character-istic individualism and consumerism, has colonised the socio-po-litical and cultural spheres in a way that, despite great gains, has spawned inequality, has disregard for the poor and the earth, and has introduced a coarsening of public discourse and a cynicism around politics and elites.

This enforced conventional wisdom – or group-think – operates out of a utilitarian, instrumental logic, subservient to the needs of the market and resistant to awkward questions about deeper val-ues and goals and the possibility of an alternative narrative. There is a loss of soul, of deeper feeling, accompanied by a culture of addiction around opioids, pornography and digital media, with alarming suicide rates. All of this points to a crisis of meaning and to what Pope Francis has called a 'globalisation of indifference'.

Christianity has resources to tackle this crisis. Its understanding of integral human development cherishes values like truth, love, justice and responsibility, as well as material well-being. It under-stands the person as intrinsically relational, and this leads naturally to an appreciation of solidarity and the common good, including an option for the poor and for the earth. All this helps enormous-ly in any attempt to re-imagine the human enterprise 'from the bottom up as well as from top down', 'from the inside out as well as the outside in'. It is time, in our pluralist society, for believers and unbelievers to learn how to pool their resources in a common attempt at re-imagining an alternative narrative.

We don't do that now. Rather, what happens is, at best, a kind of negative tolerance, an implicit contract not to interfere with the religious or secular belief of others, nor to enter into serious conversation with them about it. Can we move to a situation where we are more ready to explore and appreciate other people's religious and non-religious beliefs and practices, not in order to adopt them, but because they are important to our fellow human beings, and because they may contain important resources of social capital for the improvement our common lot? What are the challenges to Churches and unbelievers in embarking on such an approach?

The Challenge to the Catholic Church

It might be thought that the Christian Churches in Ireland have enough on their plates in terms of survival without risking the kind of partnership envisaged here. After all, in line with what has been called the 'Great Unravelling' in Western societies, including Ireland, main-line Churches are losing members as part of the individualisation and de-institutionalisation characteristic of our culture. There is the move to what Gladys Ganiel calls 'extra-institutional religion', in which religious affiliation is experienced in a less exclusive way. And for the Roman Catholic Church in particular, there is a clear sense that in the Republic of Ireland we are moving to a 'post-Catholic Ireland', due not least to the terrible clerical sexual abuse scandals.

Within this context, the temptation may be to respond in pious or managerial modes only – for example, the revival of popular devotions and the clustering of parishes – without paying sufficient attention to a more prophetic mode which would engage in dialogue with secular society. This latter mode is clearly in line with the missionary impulse outlined by Pope Francis in *Evangelii Gaudium* (2013) and elsewhere: not a plea for pity for a maligned Church, nor a proselytising pitch for new members, but a humble and yet confident appeal to the Christian tradition as service to a world that is suffering. Perhaps it is precisely at this time in Ireland, when the role of the Churches is undergoing considerable change – from institutional power to greater marginalisation in popular culture, from establishment privilege to the uncertain status of plurality – that this prophetic mode is more capable of realisation.

Archbishop Diarmuid Martin, for one, seems to be of this mind. In a recent address in an ecumenical context (2016a), he noted the challenge to all Christian Churches in an increasingly secularised Ireland to contribute to the process of the grounding of values which might inspire our modern society. Central to this challenge, he argued, was the search for a common language from the Christian tradition which makes sense to unbelievers in a pluralist society. 'The Churches urgently need to find a new language for such engagement,' he said, 'and the Churches must build bridges of new and perhaps surprising partnerships'. Charles Taylor (2007) has applied the notion of 'social imaginary' to explain that dimension of secularisation which spontaneously feels and acts without a sense of the transcendent – 'God missing but not missed' – and Martin (2016b) notes that in this dominant context faith-language becomes a foreign language to many in our society and requires translation if it is to enter into dialogue with other views. Again, he is crystal clear that he is not advocating any return to theocracy. Indeed, elsewhere (2011) he has spoken about the inevitability that the Catholic Church in Ireland would become more a minority culture, adding that 'the challenge is to ensure that it is not an irrelevant minority culture'.

There are at least two clear practical consequences for the Catholic Church if this more collaborative approach with progressive, critical secular Ireland is to take place. First, the Catholic Church itself, at hierarchical level, needs to re-imagine its role as teacher. It could be argued that it has already done so, at least in theory, by stating that conscience is primary and that morality is not to be simply identified with law. But in reality the Church continues to operate out of an anxiously paternalistic mode of moral guardianship. It needs to move to a more Socratic, midwifery mode of teaching as persuasion, in which more trust is placed in adult laity to internalise values, rather than accept applied teaching on grounds of authority alone.

This might mean that, along the lines of the 'Courtyard of the Gentiles' project initiated by Pope Benedict XVI and described by Gregory Wolfe (2013), the Catholic Church in Ireland would consider the more active promotion of conferences and public dialogues, in which prominent public intellectuals of all faiths and none would engage in conversations about human flourishing in Ireland. In this and in other ways, 'bridges of new and perhaps surprising partnerships' could be built, with the Church as part of the national dialogue we have proposed here, sometimes as initiator and sometimes as participant at the invitation of others. Interestingly, the website for the Vatican project mentioned above itself suggests that the real divide in society today is 'no longer between those who believe and do not believe in God ... but between those who recognise the gift of culture and history, of grace and gratuity, and those who found everything on the cult of efficiency, be it sacral or science.'

Secondly, as Pope Francis has clearly indicated, mission understood in this more humble sense as service to the world, demands Church reform. A Church which understands dialogue and encounter as central to mission has to embody this kind of procedure within its own organisation. To this end, Francis has proposed a kind of quiet revolution within the Catholic Church, by stating clearly that the Church for the third millennium should be 'a synodal Church', a mode of being Church which is dialogical, collegial at all levels, and in which there is an ongoing conversation and consultation between bishops, laity and theologians. It should go without saying that the unconscionable role as ascribed to women by the Catholic Church up to now needs to be urgently addressed in this conversation.

This conversation is not simply a recognition of the secular value of a more democratic organisational profile. It has deep scriptural and theological roots – in the 'sense of the faithful' of the baptised as a theological source, in the shared role of all the baptised in teaching, governance and priesthood, and in the traditional notion of the magisterium of theologians as aids to more faithful and creative episcopal teaching – all rooted in that unity and diversity imaged par excellence in God as Trinity.

For this to work, the conversation has to be open and frank as, once again, Francis has made clear. To this end, it will be helpful for the Congregation of the Doctrine of the Faith to operate in reformed mode, encouraging theological debate and intervening critically only in accordance with just procedures which are according to the canons of best contemporary practice.

This synodal mode of being Church, with its rejection of the ideology of clericalism, is of course common to other Christian Churches in Ireland and, as Francis has indicated in the case of the universal Church, the Catholic Church in Ireland can learn much of value from our fellow Christians in this respect. Without a decisive move in this direction of participation and inclusion, any attempt by the Catholic Church in Ireland to initiate dialogue with secularists will lack credibility.

Of course, the Catholic Church – in common with the other Christian Churches and indeed with other religious faiths in Ireland – has more to offer than just ideas, crucially important though these are. Post-modernity, at its best, appreciates the value of ideas but rejects the exclusive and reduced rationalism of Modernity. In this context, the Church has much to offer. There are, for example, the areas of action and witness – such as the St Vincent de Paul Society, Crosscare, Trócaire and many prophetic individuals – as well as prayer and worship, which can also be of assistance to secular society, not least with regard to rites of passage, times of celebration and grieving, and antidotes to addictive over-activity.

Finally, none of this means that the Church should stop preaching the gospel, although this will certainly involve considerable tension at times with the prevailing culture. But – again as Pope Francis has made so clear – the gospel is first and foremost about a God of love, a God who engages in human history, with huge respect for the freedom of all, who works with us for the progressive realisation of the Kingdom proclaimed by Jesus and leading to the liberation of all peoples, who has a particular care for the poor and those who suffer, and who shows great mercy for all of us who try and fail so often. It is within this overarching context that matters like teaching on sexuality and abortion take their important, if subordinate, place.

This will mean that, increasingly, the hierarchical Church will need to learn what Patrick Riordan has called (2011) the ability to speak in a polyphonic way. This implies speaking at times in the voice of unambiguous commitment to the gospel and key values, at other times speaking in the manner of measured diplomacy with compassion and understanding, while on other occasions – as we are suggesting now – signalling a willingness to cooperate and work towards improvement of what is a flawed and sinful situation. This latter voice, along with others, is characteristic of Catholic Social Teaching, with its exercise of political restraint in appealing to the language of public reason, as well as its recourse to discourse that is more properly faith-based and theological.

The Challenge to All the Churches

As already noted, the Catholic Church has much to learn from the other Christian Churches in Ireland in terms of skills and habits, and the organisational structuring of a less hierarchical, more inclusive and synodal model of Church. There is also a rich legacy of social engagement – intellectual, spiritual and practical – among Protestant Churches and groups in Ireland.

Of course, all the Christian Churches in Ireland – although not so much the less institutionally-structured Christian movements – draw largely in these days on a middle-class constituency, many of whom may well perceive that it is not in their interest to challenge the status quo. It will be part of the task for all the Churches, then, to challenge their own members to understand that the current situation is simply incompatible with gospel values, as well as being, in the longer term, arguably counter to their own self-interest. It may well be that sub-groups within the Churches may be in a better position to address this prophetic challenge more effectively.

There is a particular challenge for all the Churches in Ireland emerging from the terrible suffering of 'The Troubles'. At a personal level, there is the grieving, bitterness and resentment that are still alive in so many. At a communal level, there is ongoing sectarian division. And at a political level, the peace process needs constant safeguarding, not least as the terms of the Brexit decision are being negotiated. This situation is too easily seen by those in the Republic of Ireland as outside their remit; on the contrary, the Republic is intrinsically involved, and the Churches need to find ways of reminding their congregations that this is so. In an inter-Church document, published in 1997, the Churches were advised to operate out of a theology of solidarity and reconciliation, and to mobilise their forces accordingly. While there has been much progress in terms of good inter-Church relations at a personal level (and these are important), there has been a lack of urgency among the Churches in Ireland about finding a common voice on social issues, and a disappointing take-up of agreed ecumenical statements at the institutional level. Could there not, for example, be a more generous interpretation of current Roman Catholic guidelines with regard to Eucharistic sharing?

The Christian teaching and practice concerning grace, forgiveness and reconciliation, salvation and sin have emancipatory potential as applied to the situation on our island, North and South. This contribution will be more effectively realised when the

Churches are more fully reconciled among themselves, and when they find a common voice to speak to our society. A society which is increasingly secular will not be impressed by a divided Christian voice, whatever about a properly pluralist Christian voice.

The Challenge to Secular Society

There are plenty of reasons why even a progressively secular Ireland might want to reject this invitation to coalition, and continue with the adversarial Punch-and-Judy status quo between critical thinkers who are believers and unbelievers. There is the recent searing memory of clerical child sexual abuse, the ongoing cultural wars concerning sexual and gender issues like abortion and same-sex marriage, as well as the disputes about the continuing involvement of the institutional Church in health and education. There is, moreover, the late and rapid arrival of the Enlightenment legacy in Ireland, with its critical stance towards authority and religion. Given the close relationship of Church and State in the past, the arrival of this legacy has led to much hostility and an almost group-think rejection of Christianity and all religion. This is somewhat different to the indifference more characteristic of many other parts of Europe which have had a longer time to absorb the strengths and weaknesses of the Enlightenment.

But is not that rejection short-sighted and even, increasingly, passé? German political philosopher and public intellectual, Jürgen Habermas, one voice among many now, speaks of a 'post-secularist' Europe. In this new Europe, the presumed religious settlements in Western liberal democracies, by which religion is relegated to the private sphere along the lines of the negative tolerance I referred to above, needs to be challenged. This is because, he argues, religion has the potential to make constructive, progressive contributions to public debate. It is worth quoting him at some length about this:

> Even today, religious traditions perform the function of articulating an awareness of what is lacking or absent. They keep alive a sensitivity to failure and suffering. They rescue from oblivion the dimensions of our social and personal relations in which advances in social and cultural rationalisation have caused utter devastation. Who is to say that they do not contain *encoded semantic potentialities* (my emphasis) that could provide inspiration if only their message were translated into rational discourse and their profane truth contents were set free? (Ganiel 2016a, citing Habermas 2006).

There remains the challenge of course – for both believers and unbelievers – of making these 'encoded semantic potentialities' accessible in a post-modern culture which is mistrustful of meta-narratives and comprehensive accounts. Many believe that Habermas, for one, sets the bar too high for believers here, who risk an evacuation rather than a liberation of truth content by trying to translate their knowledge into a form of rational discourse that is arguably itself limited by exclusively and narrowly defined empirical constraints. But surely the nuances of this can be negotiated *ambulando*, through trial and error, as we engage in the conversation? Christianity, in much of its ethical thinking, is already well used to operating within the canons of 'natural reason', and this has been second nature for Catholic Social Teaching, for example, from its inception. This kind of thought and language contains an academic seriousness and wisdom and an existential concern for human flourishing that can be a great resource when allied with progressive secular thought.

But for secularists who are open to mystery – and there is mystery in all our lives, whether we are believers or unbelievers – it may be interesting to go a step further and to enquire about the 'semantic potentialities' more on their own terms, to explore the potential fruitfulness of explicitly religious and Christian discourse and symbolism for the public square. Take, for example, the notion of the intrinsic dignity of every human being, a basic tenet of Human Rights discourse that is often presumed as a 'given', without need for any grounding. It can be intriguing to observe that the Christian grounding of this conviction is not just the claim of faith that each individual human being is made in the image and likeness of God, but that this God is Trinitarian. In other words, the 'ground of our being' is not monadic, but is relational. This has enormous personal and political implications. It points to the reality that liberal individualism is only half the story, as it were, that to be an individual person is to be in relationship and that any political structure needs to account for the intrinsically social nature of personal reality.

Similarly, at this time when, despite the cult of efficiency that surrounds us, we are, if we reflect, only too aware of our own vulnerabilities and failures and rightfully fearful of dystopian social and political futures, cannot other Christian beliefs be of help? Is there not some way to liberate the powerfully symbolic and primordial realties that are spoken of in the Christian tradition in both their personal and social dimensions – grace, sin, salvation, reconciliation, history and eschatology, and so on – in such a way that might give us all, believers and unbelievers, nourishment and hope in looking the reality of our world in the eye, appreciating its beauty and yet grieving for its savagery and its suffering victims, and imagining an alternative way forward, together? In this context, Gladys Ganiel, speaking to believers, urges them to cultivate the ability to speak in secular language in the public square in order to work more productively with secular partners. But she also counsels them to use religious language too, since 'your religious tradition may furnish you with a treasure trove of inspirational stories, language, models and examples that could inspire peoples of all faiths and none' (Ganiel 2016b). Can secular dialogue partners respond generously to an invitation to conversation along these lines?

Conclusion

Pope Francis has made clear (2013) his belief that a new narrative is required to replace the neo-liberal one in which inequality is so toxic. He believes the Church is called to be 'at the service of a difficult dialogue' in which different groups of people share a common imagination and dream about a new way of living together. Francis never envisages dialogue as a mere talking shop; for him, 'realities are greater than ideas' and the talking is part of a discernment that must lead to decision and action. For this to happen, the Church needs to be reformed: he wants a synodal Church in which all voices are heard, a 'poor Church for the poor'.

Certainly, then, if he visits Ireland in 2018, this will be a different kind of papal visit from that of John Paul II in 1979. Different not only because Ireland is more secularised, but also because he has made it clear that he is not interested in an agenda which would strengthen the institutional Church with a display of power from the centre and on high. He is much more interested in the role of the Church as servant of society, in particular of the poor, a Church which can learn to be at home on the peripheries, which trusts the faith commitment and intelligence of its members and does not rely excessively and passively on hierarchical leadership, whether universal or local. It is in this context, I imagine, that Colin Murphy, could say that 'Catholics and secularists could join forces to use the papal visit to forge a new consensus: one that would prioritise the resolution of social problems and the empowerment of those who are marginalised'. This visit would be different also if, as envisaged, the Pope gets to visit Northern Ireland, a visit which could be a great symbolic boost to the peace process and to the process of reconciliation between all Christians and Churches on this island.

The temptation, in particular for the leadership of the Catholic Church, is to put all its eggs into the basket of a papal visit. This would be a terrible mistake. Papal visit or not, the dialogue between believers and unbelievers needs to take place, with all the routine and awkward difficulties that it will entail. This dialogue will require a reformed Catholic Church, as indicated, and so dialogue within the Catholic Church itself. It is we in Ireland who must do the 'heavy lifting', not the Pope.

In his Cambridge address (2011), Diarmuid Martin, more conscious than most of this need for reform, noted the daunting nature of the change required, and admitted that 'despite all my efforts I am failing in my attempts to lead such a change'. He went on to say, 'Change management has to have the patience and the strategy to bring everyone along with it and that may not be my talent'. Since that address, Pope Francis has come along and indicated very precisely what a reformed Church must look like, with dialogue and synodality at its core. Why have Diarmuid Martin and the Irish Hierarchy as a whole – with some notable exceptions – not embraced this change of direction which, if implemented, would equip the Catholic Church to enter into dialogue with secular Ireland with so much more credibility and so many more resources? It is not too late to change.

ABOUT THE AUTHORS

DAVID BEGG is Chairman of the Pensions Authority and a former General Secretary of the Irish Congress of Trade Unions. He is the author of a book on European integration and its effect on small open economies. He has a PhD in Sociology from NUI Maynooth.

MICHAEL CRONIN holds a Personal Chair in the Faculty of Humanities and Social Sciences, Dublin City University. A member of the Royal Irish Academy and the Academia Europaea, he has published widely on the subjects of language, culture and identity. He is a former Irish Language Literature Advisor to the Arts Council and Chairperson of Poetry Ireland.

ISEULT HONOHAN is Associate Professor Emeritus, UCD School of Politics and International Relations, and a Member of the Royal Irish Academy. Her research interests lie especially in the foundations of republican political theory and its application to areas including citizenship, immigration and diversity.

DERMOT A. LANE is a priest of the Dublin diocese serving in the parish of Balally. A former President of Mater Dei Institute of Education, he has taught theology for many years in Dublin and in the US. He is author and editor of a variety of publications in the areas of education and theology. He received an honorary doctorate from DCU in 2014.

DERMOT McCARTHY is a retired civil servant, having served as Secretary General to the Government and Secretary General of the Department of the Taoiseach from 2000-2011. He is now a permanent deacon in the Archdiocese of Dublin, working in the parish of St Andrew, Westland Row, Dublin.

FERGUS O'FERRALL is Lay Leader of the Methodist Church in Ireland. He has served as President of the National Youth Council of Ireland and Chairperson of The Wheel. He co-chaired the 'People's Conversation: Rethinking Citizenship for 2016'. He has been Adelaide Lecturer in Health Policy, Trinity College, Dublin and Director of The Adelaide Health Foundation. Author of several books on Irish history and public policy, he is a Governor of *The Irish Times*.

GERRY O'HANLON is a Jesuit priest, theologian and former Provincial of the Irish Jesuits. He taught for many years at the Milltown Institute, and later joined the Jesuit Centre for Faith and Justice, where he has written extensively on Church reform and the role of the Church in the public square. He has been Adjunct Professor of Theology in the Loyola Institute at Trinity College, Dublin.

REFERENCES

McCARTHY: THE SIGNS OF OUR TIMES

Francis, Pope (2013) *Evangelii Gaudium* (Dublin: Veritas) Art. 56).

Gladwell, M. (2002) *The Tipping Point: How Little Things Can Make a Big Difference* (Boston MA: Little, Brown and Company).

Higgins, President M. D. (2013) 'Toward an Ethical Economy' Available at http://www.president.ie/en/media-library/speeches/toward-an-ethical-economy-michael-d.-higgins-dublin-city-university-11th-se/

Hannon, P. (2016) 'Catholic Ireland?' *The Furrow* (October).

Humphreys, J. (2016a) 'Why Irish atheists still need the Catholic Church' *The Irish Times* (6 January) Available at https://www.irishtimes.com/opinion/joe-humphreys-why-irish-atheists-need-the-catholic-church-1.2485820

Humphreys, J. (2016b) 'How the left can rise again' *The Irish Times* (18 July) Available at https://www.irishtimes.com/opinion/joe-humphreys-how-the-left-can-rise-again-in-three-easy-steps-1.2725440/

Martin, Archbishop D. (2016a) 'The beginning of a new era' Address to Mater Dei Institute (24 August) Available at http://www.balallyparish.ie/archbishop-diarmuid-martin-the-beginning-of-a-new-era/

Martin, Archbishop D. (2016b) 'New Times Require New Institutions' Available at http://www.dublindiocese.ie/homily-at-the-final-mass-in-the-mater-dei-institute-chapel/

President of Ireland's Ethics Initiative Report (2016) *On the Importance of Ethics* Available at https://issuu.com/arasanuachtarain/docs/md_ethics_report_english_web/

The People's Conversation (2015) *Citizens Rising* Available at http://peoplesconversation.ie/citizens-rising-a-report-from-the-peoples-conversation/

White, L. Jnr (1967) 'The Historic Roots of Our Ecologic Crisis' *Science* 155: 1203-1207.

HONOHAN: RELIGIOUS PERSPECTIVES AND THE PUBLIC SQUARE

Bader, V. (2007) *Secularism or Democracy? Associational Governance of Religious Diversity* (Amsterdam: Amsterdam University Press): 266, 293.

Calhoun, C., Juergensmeyer M. & VanAntwerpen, J. (eds) (2011) *Rethinking Secularism (Oxford: Oxford University Press)*.

Carens, J. (2000) *Culture, Citizenship and Community* (Oxford: Oxford University Press).

Casanova, J. (1994) *Public Religions in the Modern World* (Chicago: University of Chicago Press).

Chassany, A. (2016) 'France: Islam and the secular state' *Financial Times* (15 September) Available at https://www.ft.com/content/05c420b8-75a5-11e6-b60a-de4532d5ea35/

Cohen, J. & Laborde, C. (eds) (2015) *Religion, Secularism, and Constitutional Democracy* (New York: Columbia University Press).

Cooke, M. (2006) 'Salvaging and Secularizing the Semantic Contents of Religion: The Limitations of Habermas's Postmetaphysical Proposal' *International Journal for Philosophy of Religion* 60 (1/3): 187-207.

Cooke, M. (2007) 'A Secular State for a Postsecular Society? Postmetaphysical Political Theory and the Place of Religion' *Constellations* 14 (2): 224-238.

Cooke, M. (2013) 'The Limits of Learning: Habermas' Social Theory and Religion' *European Journal of Philosophy* 24 (3): 694-711.

Habermas, J. (2006) 'Religion in the Public Sphere' *European Journal of Philosophy* 14 (1): 1-25.

Laborde, C. (2008) *Critical Republicanism: The Hijab Controversy and Political Philosophy* (Oxford: Oxford University Press): 40.

Laborde, C. (2017a) 'Is the liberal state secular? How much state-religion separation is necessary to secure liberal-democratic ideals' Available at http://blogs.lse.ac.uk/religionpublicsphere/2017/04/is-the-liberal-state-secular/ (accessed 20 May 2017).

Laborde, C. (2017b) *Liberalism's Religion* (Cambridge MA: Harvard University Press).

Maynor, J. (2003) *Republicanism in the Modern World* (Oxford: Polity):134.

Rougier, N. & Honohan, I. (2015) 'Religion and Education in Ireland: Growing Diversity - or Losing Faith in the System?' *Comparative Education* 51 (1): 71-86.

Sen, A. (2009) *The Idea of Justice* (Cambridge MA: Harvard University Press).

Taylor, C. (2007) *A Secular Age* (Cambridge MA: Harvard University Press).

Ungureanu, C. (2017) *Contemporary Political Philosophy and Religion* (Abingdon and New York: Routledge).

Walzer, M. (2015) *Paradox of Liberation: Secular Revolutions and Religious Counterrevolutions* (New Haven CT: Yale University Press).

Williams, R. (2012) *Faith in the Public Square* (London: Bloomsbury).

Wolterstorff, N. (2012) *Understanding Liberal Democracy: Essays in Political Philosophy* Terence Cuneo (ed.) (Oxford: Oxford University Press).

O'FERRALL: KEY AREAS FOR CONSTRUCTIVE ENGAGEMENT

Allchin, A.M. (1997) *N.F.S. Grundtvig: Introduction to His Life and Work* (London: DLT).

Bellamy, R. (2008) *Citizenship: A Very Short Introduction* (Oxford: OUP).

Berkowitz, R., Katz, J. & Keenan, T. (eds) (2010) *Thinking in Dark Times: Hannah Arendt on Ethics and Politics* (New York: Fordham University Press).

Buzzard, J. (2013) 'You need a better story' Available at www.huffingtonpost.com/justin-buzzard/you-need-a-better-story_b_3397077.html/

Crick, B. (2000) *Essays on Citizenship* (London: Continuum).

Crick, B. and Lockyer, A. (eds) (2010) *Active Citizenship: What Could It Achieve and How?* (Edinburgh: Edinburgh University Press).

Davidson, S. & Stark, A. (2011) 'Institutionalising Public Deliberation: Insights from the Scottish Parliament' *British Politics,* 6, 2: 155-186.

Honohan, Iseult (2002) *Civic Republicanism* (London: Routledge).

Mair, P. (2011) 'We need a sense of ownership of our State' in *Transforming Ireland 2011-2016: Essays from the 2011 MacGill Summer School* ed. J. Mulholland (Dublin: The Liffey Press).

Mair, P. (2013) *Ruling the Void: The Hollowing of Western Democracy* (London: Verso).

O'Ferrall, F. (2012) 'The Flourishing Society - An Overview' and 'Visioning A New Civic Republic and Building a Republican Society and State' *Towards A Flourishing Society* ed. F. O'Ferrall (Dublin: TASC).

O'Ferrall, F. (2014) 'The Civic Public Square' *Dublin Review of Books* 62 Available at http://www.drb.ie/essays/the-civic-public-square

Pettit, P. (1997) *Republicanism: A Theory of Freedom and Government* (Oxford: OUP).

Pettit, P. (2014), *Just Freedom: A Moral Compass for a Complex World* (New York: W. W. Norton & Co).

Reynolds, B. & Healy, S. (2015) *Measuring Up? Ireland's Progress: Past, Present and Future* (Dublin: Social Justice Ireland).

Sandel, M. (2009) *Justice: What's the Right Thing to Do?* (London: Penguin).

Sandel, M. (2012) *What Money Can't Buy: The Moral Limits of Markets* (New York: Farrer, Straus and Giroux).

Task Force on Active Citizenship, *Report* (2007) Available at www.wheel.ie/content/taskforce-active-citizenship/

Thaning, K. (1972) *N. F. S. Grundtvig* (Copenhagen: Det Dankse Selskab/The Danish Institute).

FOR FURTHER READING

The Report from the People's Conversation on re-thinking citizenship, entitled *Citizens Rising*, was published in 2015 by The Wheel and Carnegie UK Trust (see also www.peoplesconversation.ie).

Several Irish authors have written critiques of the Irish State and polity, describing how a civic republican vision might address the challenges confronting Irish society. Essential among these is President Michael D. Higgins, *When Ideas Matter: Speeches for an Ethical Republic* (Head of Zeus, London, 2016). Other valuable critiques include Michael D. Higgins in *Renewing the Republic* (Liberties Press, Dublin, 2011), and Peadar Kirby and Mary P. Murphy in *Towards a Second Republic: Irish Politics after the Celtic Tiger* (Pluto Press, London, 2011). The RTÉ Thomas Davis Lecture Series entitled *The Republic*, ed. Mary Jones (Mercier Press, Cork, 2005), has important essays on this topic. Fintan O'Toole in *Enough Is Enough: How to Build a New Republic* (Faber & Faber, London, 2010) and in another book edited by him, *Up the Republic! Towards a New Ireland* (Faber & Faber, London, 2012), has stimulating ideas. See also *Foundation Stone: Notes Towards a Constitution for a 21ˢᵗ-Century Republic*, ed. Theo Dorgan (New Island, Dublin, 2014) and Hugo Hamilton, Leanne O'Sullivan, Theo Dorgan and Doireann Ní Ghríofa, *Cherish Cherish Cherish: Reflections on the 1916 Proclamation* (Cork City Council, Cork, 2016).

On public deliberation, see C. F. Karpowitz, and C. Raphael, *Deliberation, Democracy, and Civic Forums* (Cambridge University Press, New York, 2014), and see also J. Gastil and P. Levine, *The Deliberative Democracy Handbook: Strategies for Effective Civic Engagement in the Twenty-First Century* (Jossey Bass, San Francisco, 2005).

LANE: ANTHROPOLOGY IN THE SERVICE OF BRIDGES TO HOPE

de Chardin, P. T. (1971) *Christianity and Evolution* (London: Collins): 227.

Foucault, M. (1970) *The Order of Things: An Archaeology of Human Science* (New York: Random House): 387.

Francis, Pope (2015a) *Laudato Si': On Care for Our Common Home* (London: CTS) Art. 68, 69, 119, 122, 118.

Francis, Pope (2015b) *Laudato Si: On Care for Our Common Home'* (London: CTS) Art 106, 210, 60.

Higgins, President M. D. (2013) 'Toward an ethical economy' Available at http://www.president.ie/en/media-library/speeches/toward-an-ethical-economy-michael-d.-higgins-dublin-city-university-11th-se

Higgins, M. D. (2015) Address to NUIG, 30 November 2015, as reported in *The Irish Times* (1 December).

Gerard Manley Hopkins (1918) 'Ribblesdale' *Poems of Gerard Manley Hopkins* (London: Humphrey, Milford).

John XXIII, Pope (1963) *Pacem in Terris* Available at http://w2.vatican.va/content/john-xxiii/en/encyclicals/documents/hf_j-xxiii_enc_11041963_pacem.html

Kavanagh, P. (1992), 'Why Sorrow?' *The Complete Poems* Patrick Kavanagh, Peter Kavanagh (Newbridge: The Goldsmith Press).

Kirwan, M. (2017) 'Theology and Education' *Vatican II and New Thinking about Catholic Education* ed. Sean Whittle (Oxford: Routledge).

Levertov, D. (1993) 'Tragic Error' *Evening Train* (New York: New Dimension Books).

Lynch, Kevin F (1965) *Images of Hope: Imagination as the Healer of the Hopeless* (Notre Dame: University of Notre Dame Press).

Ricoeur, P. (1970) 'Hope and the Structure of Philosophical Systems' *Proceedings of the American Catholic Philosophical Association*: 55-69.

Sachs, J. (2016) 'Economics for the common good' Available at www.jeff-sachs.org/2016 (accessed 17 December 2016).

Second Vatican Council (1965a) *Pastoral Constitution on the Church in the Modern World*, art. 1.

Second Vatican Council (1965b) *Pastoral Constitution on the Church in the Modern World*, art. 39, 43.

Second Vatican Council (1965c) *Pastoral Constitution on the Church in the Modern World*, art. 22.

FOR FURTHER READING

Eagleton, Terence (2015) *Hope without Optimism* (New Haven: Yale University Press).
Grey, Mary (2000) *The Outrageous pursuit of Hope: Prophetic dreams for the 21st century* (London: DLT).
Kelly, Anthony (2006) *Eschatology and Hope* (New York: Orbis Books).
Lane, Dermot A. (1966/2005) *Keeping Hope Alive: Stirrings in Christian theology* (New York: Paulist Press / Oregon: Wipf and Stock).
Lennan, Richard, and Pineda-Madrid, Nancy (eds) (2013) *Hope: Promise, Possibility, and Fulfillment* (New York: Paulist Press).

BEGG: GLOBAL ECONOMIC INSECURITY AND IRELAND'S VULNERABILITY

Begg, D. (2016) *Ireland, Small Open Economies and European Integration* (Basingstoke: Palgrave Macmillan).

Booth, S., Howarth C., Persson M., Ruparel R. & Swidlicki P. (2015) 'The Consequences, Challenges and Opportunities facing Britain outside the EU' *Open Europe Report* (London/Brussels: Open Europe).

Donovan, D. and Murphy, A. E. (2013) *The Fall of the Celtic Tiger: Ireland and the Euro Debt Crisis* (Oxford: Oxford University Press).

Fitzgerald, J. (2017) 'Recent growth owes more to Irish firms than multinationals' *The Irish Times* (26 May).

Fukuyama, F. (1992) *The End of History and the Last Man* (London: Penguin).

Gylfason, T., Holmström B., Korkman S, Söderström H.T. & Vihriäla V. (2010) *Nordics In Global Crisis: Vulnerability and Resilience* (Helsinki: The Research Institute of the Finnish Economy {ETLA}):16.

Keynes, J. M. (1936) *The General Theory of Employment, Interest and Money* (Cambridge: Macmillan).

McQuinn, K., Foley, D. & Kelly, E. (2017) *Quarterly Economic Commentary*, Spring issue (Dublin ESRI).

Mason, P. (2009) *Meltdown: The End of The Age of Greed* (London/New York: Verso): 153.

Metz, J. B. (1992) *Faith in History and Society: Towards a Practical Fundamental Theology* (New York: The Crossroads Publishing Company).

Minsky, H. P. (1986) *Stabilizing an Unstable Economy* (New York: McGraw Hill).

Munchau, W. (2016) 'Reform the economic system or the populists will do it: The interests of the financial sector and the economy at large are different' *The Financial Times* (18 December).

Paus, E. (2012) 'The Rise and Fall of the Celtic Tiger: When Deal-Making Trumps Developmentalism' *Studies in Comparative International Development*: 161-184.

Polanyi, K. (1944) *The Great Transformation: The Political and Economic Origins of our Time* (Boston: Beacon Press).

Streeck, W. (2014) *Buying Time: The Delayed Crisis of Democratic Capitalism* (London: Verso): 46.

Vallely, P. (ed) (1998) *The New Politics: Catholic Social Teaching for the Twenty-First Century* (London: SCM Press).

Wolf, M. (2014a) *The Shifts and the Shocks: What We've Learned – and Have Still to Learn – from the Financial Crisis* (London: Allen Lane): xxi.

Wolf, M. (2014b) *The Shifts and the Shocks: What We've Learned – and Have Still to Learn – from the Financial Crisis* (London: Allen Lane): xxi.

CRONIN: BEYOND THE SLOGANS: FUTURE PROSPECTS, PRESENT DILEMMAS

Anderson, K. (2015) 'The hidden agenda: how veiled techno-utopias shore up the Paris Agreement' Available at http://kevinanderson.info/blog/category/articles (accessed 10 January 2017).

Berry, T. (1999) *The Great Work: Our Way into the Future* (New York: Three Rivers Press): 67.

Brand, S. (2000) *The Clock of the Long Now: Time and Responsibility* (London: Phoenix).

Collini, S. (2012) *What Are Universities For?* (London: Penguin).

Cox, H. (2016) *The Market as God* (Cambridge MA: Harvard University Press).

Cronin, M. (2017) *Eco-Translation: Translation and Ecology in the Age of the Anthropocene* (London and New York: Routledge):94-119.

ENGIE (2016) 'COP21: Conclusions of the Climate Agreement' Available online at http://www.engie.com/en/engie-makes-climate-its-priority/cop21-conclusions-agreement (accessed 5 January 2017).

Foster, J. B. (2015) 'Marxism and Ecology: Common Fonts of a Great Transition'

Monthly Review 67.7 Available at http://monthlyreview.org/2015/12/01/marxism-and-ecology

Klein, N. (2014) *This Changes Everything: Capitalism vs. the Climate* (London: Allen Lane).

Knight, F. (1932) 'The Newer Economics and the Control of Economic Activity' *Journal of Political Economy*, 40, 4: 445-462.

Lanchester, J. (2010) *Whoops! Why Everyone Owes Everyone and No One Can Pay* (London: Penguin).

Latour, B. (2016) 'Two Bubbles of Unrealism: Learning from the Tragedy of Trump' Available at https://lareviewofbooks.org/article/two-bubbles-unrealism-learning-tragedy-trump (accessed 18 November 2016).

McKenzie Wark, K. (2015a) *Molecular Red: Theory for the Anthropocene* (London: Verso): 138.

McKenzie Wark, K. (2015b) *Molecular Red: Theory for the Anthropocene* (London: Verso): 138.

Norgaard, R. (2015) 'The Church of Economism and Its Discontents' Available at https://greattransitions.org/publication/the-church-of-economism-and-its-discontents

Oxfam International (2017) 'Just 8 men own same wealth as half the world' Available online at https://www.oxfam.org/en/pressroom/pressreleases/2017-01-16/just-8-men-own-same-wealth-half-world (accessed 16 January 2017).

Phillips, L. (2015) *Austerity Ecology and the Collapse-Porn Addicts: A Defence of Growth, Progress, Industry and Stuff* (Alresford: Zero Books).

Porter, M. & Kramer, M. (2011) 'Creating Shared Value' *Harvard Business Review* 89 1/2: 62-77.

Readings, B. (1997) *The University in Ruins* (Cambridge MA: Harvard University Press).

Raskin, P. D. (2006) *The Great Transition Today: A Report from the Future* (Boston: Tellus Institute).

Sternad, D., Kennelly, J. J. & Bradley, F. (2016a) *Digging Deeper: How Purpose-Driven Enterprises Create Real Value* (Saltaire: Greenleaf Publishing): 1-2.

Sternad, D., Kennelly, J. J. & Bradley, F. (2016b) Digging Deeper: How Purpose-Driven Enterprises Create Real Value (Saltaire: Greenleaf Publishing): 21.

World Bank Group (2016), W*orld Bank Group Climate Change Action Plan 2016-2020* (Washington DC: World Bank) Available online at https://www.openknowledge.worldbank.org/handle/10986/24451

O'HANLON: A CHALLENGE TO THE CHURCHES

Department of Theological Questions of the Irish Inter-Church Meeting (1997) *Freedom, Justice and Responsibility in Ireland Today* (Dublin: Veritas).

Francis, Pope (2013) *Evangelii Gaudium* (Dublin: Veritas).

Francis, Pope (2015) *Laudato Si': On Care for Our Common Home* (Dublin: Veritas).

Ganiel, G. (2016a) *Transforming Post-Catholic Ireland* (Oxford: OUP): 242.

Gamiel, G. (2016b) *Transforming Post-Catholic Ireland* (Oxford: OUP): 254.

Lonergan, B. J. F. (1970) *Insight: A Study of Human Understanding* (New York: Philosophical Library) Chapters 6, 7 (3rd edition: first published 1957).

Martin, Archbishop D. (2011) 'Keeping the show on the road: Is this the future of the Irish Catholic Church?' available at http://www.dublindiocese.ie/content/22022011-cambridge-group-irish-studies

Martin, Archbishop D. (2016a) 'Sermon at the Ecumenical Choral Evensong in Christ Church, Dublin' (13 Nov.) Available at www.dublindiocese.ie/category/archbishops-talks-and-addresses

Martin, Archibishop D. (2016b) 'Reflections of Archbishop Diarmuid Martin, Archbishop of Dublin, at the Irish Catholic Conference on "The Future of Faith Based Schools in a Secular Society"' (20 Oct) Available at www.catholicbishops.ie/2016/10/20/reflections-of-archbishop-diarmuid-martin

Murphy, C. (2016) 'Ten ways the Pope's visit can help us examine our national history and psyche' *The Sunday Business Post* (4 December).

Riordan, P. (2011) 'A Blessed Rage for the Common Good' *Irish Theological Quarterly*, 76 1: 3-19.

Taylor, C. (2007) *A Secular Age* (Harvard University Press).

Wolfe, G. (2013) 'Courtyard of the Gentiles' *Image Journal* Available at https://imagejournal.org/issue/issue76

FOR FURTHER READING

O'Hanlon, Gerry (2010) *Theology in the Irish Public Square* (Dublin: Columba)